DEAR WOMAN

Get Well Letters of Hope

Chavos Buycks

Dear Woman: Get Well Letters of Hope
Copyright © 2015 by Chavos Buycks
Published by Ear To Hear Publishing™
www.eartohearbooks.com

Unless otherwise indicated, all Scripture quotations are taken from the New King James Version® (NKJV). Copyright © 1982 by Thomas Nelson, Inc.

Scripture quotations marked NLT are taken from the Holy Bible, New Living Translation, copyright ©1996, 2004, 2007 by Tyndale House Foundation. Used by permission of Tyndale House Publishers, Inc., Carol Stream, Illinois 60188. All rights reserved.

Scripture quotations marked CJB are taken from the Complete Jewish Bible by David H. Stern. Copyright © 1998. All rights reserved. Used by permission of Messianic Jewish Publishers, 6120 Day Long Lane, Clarksville, MD 21029. www.messianicjewish.net.

Scripture quotations marked MSG are taken from The Message. Copyright © 1993, 1994, 1995, 1996, 2000, 2001, 2002. Used by permission of NavPress Publishing Group.

Scripture quotations marked NIV are taken from THE HOLY BIBLE, NEW INTERNATIONAL VERSION®, NIV® Copyright © 1973, 1978, 1984, 2011 by Biblica, Inc.® Used by permission. All rights reserved worldwide.

Scripture quotations marked TLB are taken from The Living Bible copyright © 1971 by Tyndale House Foundation. Used by permission of Tyndale House Publishers Inc., Carol Stream, Illinois 60188. All rights reserved.

Printed in the United States.

ISBN 978-0-9861935-0-7

All rights reserved. This book is protected by the copyright laws of the United States of America. This book may not be copied or reprinted for commercial gain or profit. This book or parts thereof may not be reproduced in any form, except for brief quotations in reviews, without written permission from the author and publisher. If you have any questions, please contact info@eartohearbooks.com.

This book is dedicated to every woman who has dealt with or knows a woman who has endometriosis or any other chronic illness.

Contents

Disclaimer		6
Introduction: *My Life Is a Letter*		7

I. The Spirit of Infirmity

Letter 1	Endometri-What?	13
Letter 2	Pain, Pain, Go Away	17
Letter 3	I'm Tired of Crying	21
Letter 4	Held in Prison	25
Letter 5	Oh Boy, Aunt Flo Is Here	29
Letter 6	Lord, I Hate My Period	33
Letter 7	My Friend Named Fear	37
Letter 8	Thorn in My Flesh	41
Letter 9	Paralyzed By Endo	45

II. Eighteen Years

Letter 10	Discouraged Avenue	51
Letter 11	Childbearing Years	55
Letter 12	Doctor, Doctor	59
Letter 13	It's All in Your Head	63
Letter 14	The Waiting Room	67
Letter 15	Bad Reports	71
Letter 16	I'm a Barren Mess	75
Letter 17	Why Have You Forsaken Me?	79
Letter 18	God, I'm Angry With You	83

III. Could No Wise Lift Herself Up

Letter 19	I'm So Weak	91
Letter 20	I Give Up	95
Letter 21	Lord, Carest Thou Not?	97
Letter 22	Lord, Help My Unbelief	101
Letter 23	I'm PMSing	105
Letter 24	Shame, Shame, Shame	109

Letter 25	God Must Be Mad At Me	113
Letter 26	Please, No More Suffering	117
Letter 27	New Mercies	121

IV. Seen By Jesus

Letter 28	Daughter of Abraham	127
Letter 29	Dear Woman	131
Letter 30	Jesus Sees You	135
Letter 31	Jesus Calls You	139
Letter 32	The Lord of The Sabbath	143
Letter 33	The Stripes of Jesus	147
Letter 34	Under His Wings	151
Letter 35	You're on His Mind	155

V. Woman Thou Art Loosed

Letter 36	Friends of Faith	161
Letter 37	He Touched Me	167
Letter 38	Loose Me and Let Me Go	171
Letter 39	Rest a While	175
Letter 40	Peace, Be Still	179
Letter 41	Punk Your Period	183
Letter 42	Stand Up Straight	189
Letter 43	Praise Is What I Do	193
Letter 44	Take Up Your Mat and Walk	197
Letter 45	Strong Woman	201
Letter 46	Them Fighting Words	205
Letter 47	Fight Like a Lady	209
Letter 48	Woman of Faith	215
Letter 49	The End of Endo	219
Letter 50	Worship in the Warfare	223
Letter 51	Most Wanted	227
Letter 52	Victorious Woman	231

Notes — 235
Top Supporters List — 238
Acknowledgments — 239
About the Author — 241
What's Next — 242

Disclaimer:

This is my personal story, and it is not intended to replace seeking professional medical assistance for your situation. Some identifying details (i.e. names, dialogue and events) have been changed.

Thank you for reading my story, and I hope you are encouraged.

Introduction

My Life Is a Letter

Dear *Woman*,

Who doesn't like going to the mailbox and getting a handwritten letter from a friend? If I could, I would've handwritten each letter to you in this book. But I don't want your eyes to hurt from straining to figure out what my not-so-pretty handwriting means. So, the closest thing that is readable, easy on the eyes, and nice-looking is to stick with typing it out. ☺

Think of this devotional memoir as a paper mailbox you can visit daily, weekly or biweekly to read fifty-two hope-filled letters from me, your new pen pal. It's up to you. There are three interactive features at the end of each letter: a prayer, a meditation with a phrase or scripture and a tip to help you stand. These come out to represent the acronym (PMS).

I am open, honest, transparent, and raw in these letters about my journey living with my personal storm of Stage IV endometriosis. I was diagnosed in 2009 with endometriosis, but had symptoms since 2004.

For those who might not know what endo is, *endometriosis (aka endo) is an invisible debilitating gynecological condition, where displaced endometrium tissue of the uterus shows up on the outside of the uterus. The displaced tissue bleeds each month during the menstrual cycle causing the woman to have two periods— one inside the uterus and one outside the uterus.*

I talk with you in these letters like we're sitting face to face drinking tea or on the phone. I share about this very intimate and hard season of my life— one of the greatest storms I've ever been in.

During one of my endo-storms, I was in desperate need of encouragement, hope and comfort. I grabbed my white laptop to search for a book to encourage me and to speak to my condition.

At the time, I only found health-related materials on endometriosis, not a single memoir or devotional from a woman, who'd battled with endo herself.

I did find a book by a woman, who had been diagnosed with cancer, and the idea came to my mind: "Why not write your own devotional?"

This devotional is for women dealing with a chronic illness, or maybe an impending divorce, depression, financial struggles, shame, etc.

The title of this book, *Dear Woman*, was inspired by the woman in Luke 13. The Bible doesn't reveal her name to us, but we can see she is in the midst of her storm of life.

> "One Sabbath day as Jesus was teaching in a synagogue, he saw a woman who had been crippled by an evil spirit. She had been bent double for eighteen years and was unable to stand up straight. When Jesus saw her, he called her over and said, "Dear woman, you are healed of your sickness!" Then he touched her, and instantly she could stand straight. How she praised God." (Luke 13:13 NLT).

I've become well acquainted with the "Dear Woman's" story. I interweave my story with hers. Her story is broken up in five parts: first, we see the revealing of her storm of life (i.e. sickness). Second, we see the length she's been dealing with it for eighteen years. Third, we see her condition in how she's unable to care for herself. Fourth, we see Jesus intervene in the midst of her storm. Fifth, we see the result and impact Jesus had on the Dear Woman's condition.

The fifty-two letters in this book fall under those five sections. You will see how I found out about endometriosis and my response to it. You will see my thoughts and struggles, through this endo-storm. You will see how I relate to God in the midst of my storm. You will see my action and fight to stay strong in the storm. As I share, I pray you can find hope and encouragement as you read these letters.

I also share about others who were in their storms of life: like Jesus's disciples, Paul, Job, David, the woman with the issue of blood, Hannah, and more. Their responses and attitudes in their storms will encourage you to know that your feeling of anger, depression, disappointment, unbelief, fear, shame, isolation, or hopelessness is normal. And it's about how God came in and aided and strengthened them in their storm. He will do the same for you in your storm.

Introduction: My Life Is a Letter

If you or someone you know has a chronic illness, especially endometriosis, and has been suffering for years with pain, this book is for you.

If you are discouraged, weary, depressed, or overwhelmed, this book is for you.

If you've ever felt forsaken by God or maybe angry with Him, this book is for you.

If you enjoy reading memoirs, overcoming stories and devotionals, this book is for you.

My desire is to encourage and give a word of comfort to help you on your journey. Whatever storms of life you're facing right now, be encouraged, you are not alone. You have a friend of faith cheering you on, "You can make it!"

You have a God, who sees you and is cheering you on. He says, "You will make it! You have overcome!" This book is my letter to you, my sister. "*Dear Woman*, you are victorious!"

I. The Spirit of Infirmity

LETTER 1

Endometri -What?

"The name of the Lord is a strong tower; the righteous run to it and are safe."
~King Solomon (Proverbs 18:10).

Dear *Woman*,

My sister is a doctor. Well...not really, but she should be. She's the one who diagnosed me. I know that sounds strange, but it's true.

Okay, let me tell you what happened.

It was the fall of 2009. I was relaxing with my gadget-savvy husband, Garry, at our loft apartment (previously an old cigar-manufacturing building in downtown Kansas City). I was growing tired of the painful cramps and nausea episodes breaking in and interrupting my life, my stomach and my marriage.

I sat at the breakfast bar on my favorite silver-and-black swivel stool with my hands over my face. I said, "Why am I going through this? I'm tired of dealing with this." My phone rang, and I answered.

My sister Vonna greeted me in her Ms. Piggy sisterly tone, "Hi Vozzie."

I doubled over against the pain and laid my head on the breakfast bar. "Hey Vonna, what's up?"

"Nothing, what're you doing?"

"Nothing much." A wave of hot nausea washed over my face, down my neck. "Just sitting here with Garry."

"You sound a little winded," Vonna said.

"Oh no, I'm fi— HOLD ON." I sprinted to the bathroom, and made it with seconds to spare. My breakfast decided to revisit.

Back to the phone. "How you doing, Vonna?"

Somewhere during our conversation I blurted, "I've been vomiting, having diarrhea, bad cramps and pain on my periods."

"What? You've been vomiting on your periods. For how long?" Vonna no longer had that sisterly Ms. Piggy tone with me. It was more a concerned and motherly tone.

"Ever since I got married in 2004." At the time of this conversation, I had been dealing with these symptoms for more than four years, and it was normal to me. I didn't think it was a big deal, just a part of being a woman. So when Vonna got all up in my face about it, I thought *maybe something wasn't completely right.*

"Chavos, that's not normal!" Vonna raised her voice a few notches.

"Well, it's normal for me. For as long as I can remember."

"I mean it's not healthy." Vonna sounded serious. Still bossy, but now serious. "Have you ever heard of endometriosis?"

Swirling around on my stool, "Endo-metri-what?" I thought: what the heck is that word, and how does my little baby sister know about it.

"Endo-metri-o-sis, it sounds like that's what you might have. You should look it up. Love you Vozzie," Vonna said in her Ms. Piggy sisterly tone.

That evening, I pulled out my white laptop to search out my newfound word. I typed "what is endometriosis" in the Google search bar, and a wealth of information popped up. I fit every last symptom I read. "Vonna was right!" I said out loud.

I found out that *176 million plus* women are affected by endometriosis. I was shocked and surprised. That's a lot of women, and now I was a part of that number (so was my mother), and I'd had no idea.

I slammed my laptop closed and spun around from the breakfast bar. I jumped off my black stool, and shouted to my husband, "WHY DIDN'T ANYONE TELL ME THIS? After all these years since we got married in 2004 I never knew what was wrong with me. And I had to find out from my sister, not a doctor. I can't believe this!"

You see before this conversation, I was going to a Women's Clinic for a year and half for nausea, and no nurse or doctor ever diagnosed me with this condition. The nurse prescribed medication to help with the nausea, but it made me drowsy, dizzy and unable to function at work and home. It wasn't helpful at all. But I was thankful to find out when I did.

I finally understood what was going on in my body. I had no idea that the conversation with my sister "the doctor" would change my life.

After that conversation, I began to search for another Women's Clinic. I found one with a great OB-GYN, who jumped right on my situation. She confirmed my sister's diagnosis and everything I'd looked up.

After several years of dealing with endometriosis I came across Luke 13. It talks about this woman (a dear woman), who was crippled by a spirit of infirmity. *That's it, the root of my endometriosis is a spirit of infirmity.* I could identify with her and the other woman in the Bible, who had an issue of blood for twelve years. To think of endometriosis as a spirit of infirmity made it sound like I was possessed or something. I decided I'd rather stick with the name endometriosis. But either way, it's just another name for the same painful problem.

Endometriosis is a strange-looking name. Half the time I misspell it. I came to understand this one thing: no matter the name, endometriosis and any spirit of infirmity must bow at the name of Jesus. This is good news.

If you have endometriosis, how did you find out? From a doctor? A friend? A teacher? Google? However you found out, there is hope. If Jesus dealt with a spirit of infirmity for the *"dear woman"* (in Luke 13), then He's well able to deal with it in my body and yours, too.

Here's what I'm asking God...

God, endometriosis is the name of a disease, and that name (and the name of any other illness) isn't greater than the name of Jesus. Help me to remember this in the midst of the uncomfortable and painful symptoms. I give honor to Your name and say Your name is greater than all other names under heaven and earth. Your name is a great and strong tower for me to run into and find safety. I declare Your name, Lord Jesus, is above every name, and every knee must bow. Endometriosis (name your illness) must bow at the name, Jesus.

Here's something to think on...

Every knee will bow and pay homage to King Jesus. (Philippians 2: 8-11).

Here's a tip to help you stand...

For fun: See how many ways you can misspell endometriosis or your chronic illness? Or how many words can you find within that name? For example: There are 920 words within the name "endometriosis." Create a sentence, a song, a poem or a movie title using those words you find. Have fun! (My movie title— "Meet Miss Modest Dress")

LETTER 2

Pain, Pain, Go Away

"Our glory is hidden in our pain, if we allow God to bring
the gift of Himself in our experience of it." [1]

~Henri Nouwen

Dear *Woman*,

You may be experiencing pain in your body right now or may have suffered in the past. I'm familiar with pain. I've experienced the horrible pelvic pain and debilitating cramps that come with having endo. The pain was so bad at times, it felt like someone had karate-kicked me in the stomach, and I was going to die. There were days I couldn't take it anymore. All I could do was cry out to God for relief.

Some months I'd get a break, but it would come back stronger the next. My song was, "Pain, Pain Go Away, please don't come back another day." Have you ever sung that song?

You might not understand why you're going through this and experiencing so much pain. I sure didn't understand why before I learned about endometriosis. I love people, and I bet you do, too. You give of yourself. You serve. You do the best you can do. You strive to live a godly life before your God. Yet month after month, you are in pain with no relief. You hope the pain will just go away.

Have you heard of the story of Job? This poor guy experienced one pain after another (see the Book of Job). It all started after God asked the enemy,

"Have you considered my servant Job?" I could hear the same conversation over my life, God asking, "Have you considered my daughter?" Well God, please don't consider me, would be my next thought. But why not me? Why not Job?

Job lost his children and his health, and his wife lost her mind by telling Job to curse God and die. Why in the world would she tell her husband, whom she loved so dearly, to 'go off' on God, and while you're at it go ahead and die? Why didn't she as a loving wife encourage him? She could've said, "Job, I know you're in pain right now, but we're going to make it through this together. We know God, so let's pray to him. I don't want you to die."

Poor guy, it wasn't enough that he had to deal with the gates of hell coming against him. He had to deal with his crazy wife in one ear and his insensitive friends in the other ear, calling him a sinner. And all of this on top of being in extreme pain with boils covering his whole body; it's no wonder he eventually cursed the day he was born.

You and I can relate to experiencing pain minute after minute, day after day, month after month. At times, the pain can cause us to long for the grave. Job got to that point, too. Why the abundance of pain for Job? Why the abundance of pain for you? Maybe he did something wrong? No, he did nothing wrong. Even though Job's friends were convinced he had sinned *big time*.

I didn't have friends like Job in my ear, telling me I've sinned. I had thoughts in my head that whispered, "You did something wrong." I agreed, "Yeah, maybe I'm going through this because I did such-and-such as a teenager, and now I'm paying for it." That thought tormented me like Job's well-meaning friends did him. Have you experienced accusatory thoughts like this before? Have you thought your pain was payment? It's not true. Your pain is not a punishment for something you've done or didn't do. You're not experiencing this pain because you sinned.

What if you are going through this Job-experience not because you've sinned, but because you have been righteous in God's eyes? What? That's crazy, I know, but what if that's the case. It was certainly the case for Job.

God said, "He (Job) was a blameless and upright man." (Job 1:8). Although he was a righteous man, Job was in a lot of pain. All the pain he experienced was not in vain. At the end of his story Job received double for all he went through. Double! If it happened for Job, then I must believe it will happen for me and for you. We will receive double for all we have lost and gone through. Double! God will restore the years endometriosis and any other illness has taken from my life, your life, your family, your body and your mind. He will restore! God restored Job, and he was better than he was before he went through his suffering.

You will be, too. You will have more. I know it doesn't seem like it right now, and it may be hard to see. In the beginning of my journey, it was hard for me to see how God would turn it for my good, too. But He will because you love him, and you are called according to His purpose.[2]

And when it's all done, you will be able to do what James says, "Count it all joy." (James 1:2). Job was able to count it all joy in the end of his pain and suffering. I am able to count it all joy now, but not while I'm going through it. It took many years for me to get to this place, and at times I still forget. And you might not be able to do this in the midst of your pain or suffering right now, and that's okay. But hold on till the end, and believe that Jesus stands over your situation and says, "Pain, Pain Go Away, don't come back any day, for I took her pain in my body so that she will experience healing and relief."

Here's what I'm asking God...

God, cause me to experience comfort and relief from pain this very moment, and for the days and months to come. Send Holy Spirit, the Comforter, for I need him desperately to comfort me. Let me receive double as a good friend of Job, one that has experienced pain and discomfort. See me as righteous in Your eyes. Comfort me, O God, Your daughter. Help me in the end to be able to count it all joy. Bring peace and comfort to my mind, body and soul. I declare pain, cramps, backaches and headaches to leave my body in the name of Jesus. I exchange my pain for Jesus's healing.

Here's something to think on...

The Lord blessed the latter end of Job even more than the beginning. (Job 42:12).

Here's a tip to help you stand...

Take some doctor-approved painkillers and sleep. Or if you feel up to it, find a good comedy show or movie and LAUGH. (I like AFV, The Cosby Show, Thou Shalt Laugh, and comedians: Michael Jr and Sinbad). Laugh until you cry and your stomach hurts for a good reason.☺

LETTER 3

I'm Tired of Crying

"It is such a secret place, the land of Tears." [3]
~Antoine de Saint-Exupery

Dear *Woman*,

I cry like a girl, and there is nothing wrong with that since that is what I am—a grown-up girl. But sometimes I've cried so much that I didn't think I had any tears left. I would lay in my bed, and tears would drop from my face like rain falling out of the sky and puddling on my fluffy white pillow. I was so tired of crying about being sick and having endometriosis that one day I decided, "I'm not shedding one more tear about this. I'm done!"

Somewhere, along the way I began to believe the lie that says, "It's not okay to cry about the same issue over and over." The lie that says, "It's bad to cry." The lie that says, "I need to suck it up and just deal with it." The lie that says, "I'm weak if I cry."

Crying reminded me that I was broken, and this illness was still around. Little did I know that God is not intimidated by my tears, and He doesn't think my crying like a girl is bad. So why did I condemn myself when He didn't condemn me?

When babies cry, we tend to them and care for them. Their tears signify to us that something is wrong, and they need or want something. We will take a tissue and wipe their tears, but we don't collect them or jot them down on a sheet every time they cry.

God is my Father, and He tends to my cry. Our crying and tears signify to God that we are in need of His help. The Bible tells us that, "The rigtheous cry out, and the Lord hears, And delivers them out of all their troubles." (Psalm 34:17).

Not only does He hear them, David said to God, "You keep track of all my sorrows. You have collected all my tears in your bottle. You have recorded each one in your book." (Psalm 56:8). Did you know your tears and mine are heavenly collectible items? Yep. Our tears are precious *collectible items* by God and featured in His book. Whoa! So, the times I decided not to cry and let my tears flow, they weren't collected, nor were they recorded in God's book. What an honor and privilege to have the One who runs the universe be concerned about our tears.

David was familiar with sorrow, sadness and suffering. He wrote: "I am weary with my groaning; all night I make my bed swim; I drench my couch with my tears." (Psalm 6:6). He also said: "I am weary with my crying; my throat is dry; my eyes fail while I wait for my God." (Psalm 69:3). Yet, he was okay with shedding tears even as a King of Israel. He cried like a man. A kingly man. He knew how precious his tears were and that God heard the cries of his people even when we think He has in earplugs.

Have you ever decided that you were not going to shed one more tear? It's okay to shed tears. This is the way we were created. God hears our cries and collects are tears. Tears are normal. Tears are good. Tears are precious. Go ahead, and cry like a girl. Let your tears fall and fill your pillow with puddles. Daddy God will catch them as they fall.

I'm Tired of Crying

Here's what I'm asking God...

God, hear the voice of my crying. Don't turn a deaf ear to my weeping. I cry to You! Catch my tears as they fall, and collect them in your bottle, and record them in Your book for they are many. Hear my cry, O Lord, and tend unto my prayer. I declare the Lord hears the cries of the righteous and delivers them out of all their troubles.

Here's something to think on...

There is a promise to us who have sown in tears. We shall reap in joy.
(Psalm 126:5).

Here's a tip to help you stand...

Grab a box of tissue, and let the tears flow; for every tear put a penny in a glass bottle. Or if you like to draw, draw tears inside a bottle and label the bottle as a memorial of what each tear represents.

LETTER 4

Held in Prison

"Therefore if the Son makes you free, you shall be free indeed."
~Jesus (John 8:28).

Dear *Woman*,

I'm a woman behind bars. I'm behind prison bars even though I can walk freely. I'm not confined to a physical prison, but healthwise I'm in prison. I'm held captive by chains of affliction.

And I'm not the only one that has felt this way. The *"dear woman"* (in Luke 13) was in prison, too. It wasn't because she committed a misdemeanor that she was held in prison. There is no explanation given why she was held in prison. It must not have been that important to know the *why*, but it was important to know she was a daughter of Abraham and in prison.

It is not fitting for a daughter of Abraham—the father of faith and a friend of God—to be in prison. This was wrong. How dare anyone put her behind bars for an unjust cause? How would it look to put the daughter of the President of the US or of a prince or a king behind bars? It doesn't fit, a princess in prison. Jesus stated this fact about her being a daughter of Abraham for a reason; it must have been important to know who she was. He knew who she was and that she shouldn't be held in bondage. He walked into the synagogue that day, and it was filled with His presence. The Bible says, "Where the Spirit of the Lord is there is freedom." (2 Corinthians 3:17 NLT). For this daughter of Abraham, on that day Jesus brought freedom.

He was on an Isaiah 61 mission to set at liberty those who were captive, and He did just that for this *"dear woman."* She had been held in prison for eighteen years before being released.

I don't know what number you are on with dealing with your illness—whether it has been a week, a month, six months, a year, five years, ten years or more. Jesus's mission has been and still is to set people free from their captivity.

I've been in prison, in chains of affliction for almost ten years. Year after year, I waited for freedom from endometriosis, for the illness to be loosed from my body. The more I'd pray, the chains of affliction got tighter and tighter, making it unbearable to deal with life.

It is not easy, but now I praise God while in my chains. I'm on a journey to know liberation from my chains of affliction. I'm a daughter of the King of Kings, and it isn't right for me to be held in prison without just cause. Jesus is my Liberator. He specializes in releasing captives from their bondage and chains of afflictions.

He is a Deliverer. There would be no need for a Deliverer or Liberator if there wasn't captivity or bondage. In the end, when it is all over, I will know Him as the *Great Deliverer* and *Liberator* and experience freedom, knowing Him as the Son who sets free.

Do you feel like you're in chains of affliction? Are you held in prison by endometriosis, cancer, or something else? If you feel the chains of affliction holding on with a tight squeeze, trying to choke the life and joy out of you, He comes as a *Great Liberator*, and where the Spirit of the Lord is, there is freedom![4] His Spirit is alive in you, moving inside your body no matter how you feel or how the circumstances look. We can be free even in the midst of our chains of affliction. He comes as the Joy-Giver in the midst of trials.

There is a song by William Reagan (performed by Tasha Cobbs), which I believe is fitting for those of us in chains of affliction. Will you sing this song with me today? It goes like this,

> *"There is power in the name of Jesus*
> *There is power in the name of Jesus*
> *There is power in the name of Jesus*

Held in Prison

> *To break every chain*
> *Break every chain*
> *Break every chain*
>
> *I hear the chains falling*
> *I hear the chains falling."* [5]

I declare over us, I see and hear those chains of affliction falling. There is freedom in the name of Jesus, to break every chain, break every chain. There is freedom in the name of Jesus, to break every chain of affliction, break every chain of illness. Freedom reigns in you. The *Son* lives in you, and who the Son sets free is *free* indeed![6]

Here's what I'm asking God...

Jesus, You're the great liberator. You set at liberty those who are captive. Release me from the chains of affliction and bondage and from this spirit of infirmity just as You did for the "*dear woman*" (in Luke 13). Give me the grace and strength to praise You while in the midst of trials and chains like Paul and Silas did in their chains. I declare, I will walk in freedom because the Son has set me free.

Here's something to think on...

The Lord's presence brings freedom. (2 Corinthians 3:17; Acts 16:25-26).

Here's a tip to help you stand...

Listen to "*Break Every Chain*" by Tasha Cobbs on YouTube. While you listen to it, see Jesus, the Son of God, taking the key of freedom and unlocking the chains of affliction. Do a freedom dance and shout a freedom song. Let freedom reign in and through you.

LETTER 5

Oh Boy, Aunt Flo Is Here

"Aunt Flo don't you know you should be kind all the time."
~Chavos B.

Dear *Woman*,

When my aunt comes for a visit, I want to run the other way. Do you have a favorite relative? Like a favorite aunt, uncle or cousin you love to see and any chance you have you make sure to see them when they're in town, you wouldn't mind them dropping by your house for an unannounced visit.

However, what about that not-so favorite relative? When they come around you dodge them, saying, "Oh boy, aunt or uncle so-and-so is here." You go to another room just to avoid them. You're not at all excited to hear they're in town, and you surely do mind if they dropped in for a quick visit. This is how I feel about Aunt Flo; she is my least favorite.

This is how her visits usually go down. She arrives promptly on schedule each month around the 25th day. She must really like that date. Her very presence makes me lose everything I ate that day. She carries heavy luggage with her that almost breaks my back and causes a lot of stress and headaches. Oh, did I mention she always brings her mean twin pets named "Pain and Cramps."

She demands I give her all my time and attention and attend to her every need. I'm on the couch or in bed most of the visit because I'm out of gas; she makes sure to totally zap me dry of all strength like kryptonite on Superman. She is annoying and not a joy to have around at all. I dread her visits and look forward to her quick departure. She stays for five days, but as soon as she leaves I immediately begin to count the days until her next visit.

I prayed for years for Aunt Flo not to come, or at least for her visits to be pleasant and sweet and her luggage to be light. I've asked for her to be a joy and not a pain or to cause headaches. Why can't she be a sweet aunt? Why is she so evil at times? She's snappy and unstable. She might be happy one moment and sad the next. She challenges me month after month, making me stronger with each visit.

How is your experience when Aunt Flo visits or used to visit? Does she bring her heavy luggage that almost breaks your back? Is her visit similar to what I described? What about her pets, "pain and cramps?" If so, you are stronger because of her visits, too.

Just hold on, she'll be gone in a very few days, and yes, she'll be back again. But don't fret, you were built to endure these light afflictions that are but for a moment. May God cause you to have sweet and enjoyable times with your new "favorite" aunt month after month.

Oh Boy, Aunt Flo is Here

Here's what I'm asking God...

God, You see all the headaches, pain and challenges I go through with Aunt Flo's visit each month. Satisfy my soul during these visits with the sweetness of Your presence and the honey of Your word. Release endurance and grace over me. Cause her visits to be pleasant, sweet and light. Help me to not despise her, but enjoy her. I declare times of refreshing will come from the presence of the Lord. (Acts 3:19).

Here's something to think on...

These light afflictions don't measure up to eternity. (2 Corinthians 4:17).

Here's a tip to help you stand...

Survive her visit: Keep calm. Breathe. Play some nice music. Put your feet up and rest. Stock up on dark chocolate.*

*Fun fact: Dark chocolate can help with mood swings and boost serotonin.

LETTER 6

Lord, I Hate My Period

*"Out of the same mouth proceed blessing and cursing.
My brethren, these things ought not to be so."
~James (James 3:10).*

Dear *Woman*,

I hate my period. I didn't always feel that way. Can you believe there was a time as a young girl I desired and even prayed for my period to come? I know that sounds crazy, but it's true. Girls younger than me started their periods before I did. My younger sister was one of those girls; she started her period at age twelve. I checked everyday to see if I started, so anxious for it to come.

My sweet granny said, "Be patient, and it will come."

I waited for its arrival like a person at the bus-stop. And I prayed, "Lord, please, let my period start." After several months, it finally arrived when I was fourteen, and I was so excited to finally have a period. I was no longer a little girl; I had crossed over into womanhood. At fourteen I had no idea what awaited me.

Many years later that excitement turned into dislike, and the dislike turned into hatred. My hatred toward my period was often voiced to my husband with disdain. I would say, "I hate my period." My periods felt like a life sentence. I know this wasn't God's original intent for me, but at times I thought I was being punished for something. I now dreaded my once-prayed-for period. Oh, if I really knew what I was asking God.

There came a time when God revealed to me, "Every time you speak that you hate your period, you are actually cursing it." The hatred for my period was a form of self-rejection of the way the Creator made me. And what I really meant was, "God, what were you thinking, making me a woman? You made me flawed."

This is not what He desired for me. His desire was for me to be blessed and to be thankful to Him for my periods. To see it as He sees it: a God-ordained system for cleansing and to enable me to reproduce and become a mother.

God created me as a woman and along with my periods, He saw and said, "*It was good*" (Genesis 2:31). Who was I, the creation, to say otherwise? It was a struggle because I couldn't agree that it was good. I had the wrong perspective because it didn't feel good all the time, so how could it be good?

I have a new mindset about my periods now. But at first, it was a difficult task to make my mouth bless and thank God for my periods when I felt completely different. I began to see my periods not as a life sentence anymore, but as one of the many things that marks my womanhood. It is a limited avenue for pregnancy that will end one day.

I switched from hatred to saying, "God, I thank you for making me a woman, and I thank you for my periods." And I believe it is good for me to have them, and for you too, if you are in your childbearing years. And when it's time for me to enter menopause by God's perfect design, it will be all good, too. We are God's beautiful creation—woman. We are a *"good thing."* [7]

Here's what I'm asking God...

God, I will not strive with You my Master, nor will I (like clay) say to You who formed me: "What are you making?" You are the Potter, and You're certainly greater than me, the clay. I am the work of Your hands. All that Your hands have created (the world, creatures, man, woman, my periods, my body), You've called, "*good*." Cause me to come into agreement with that statement when my feelings and my body scream otherwise. Thank You for making me one of Your most beautiful creations—woman and all that comes with being a woman. For woman is the glory of man. (1 Corinthians 11:7). I declare: I will bless what God blesses.

Here's something to think on...

You are a beautiful masterpiece created by the hand of God.
(Psalm 139:14).

Here's a tip to help you stand...

Write a thank you card to God for being a woman (include your period, body, personality, etc.). If you're bold, look in the mirror and finish the sentence: I'm glad to be a woman because...pick a feature and compliment yourself.

LETTER 7

My Friend Named Fear

"For God has not given us a spirit of fear, but of power and of love and of a sound mind."
~Apostle Paul (2 Timothy 1:7).

Dear *Woman,*

I'm such a scaredy cat. I get it from my friend, who is a scaredy cat, too. I guess it's true: "Birds of a feather do flock together." Her name is Fear. She is afraid of everything.

In the past, we hung out together often. We were really close. I took advice from her all the time, hanging onto her lies and every doubtful and scary word she spoke. Her words led me into darkness and despair. They got louder and stronger right before Aunt Flo was due for a visit. She would say, "Oh, you know Aunt Flo is coming. You better gear up for the rough ride. How many days is it until she arrives?"

Reaching for my cell phone, I opened up the calendar app, and starting at the last day of my last period, I would count, "One, two, three, four, five," all the way to the 25th or 28th day. I thought, "This is the day it's going down," as I tapped the screen.

I *kicked* it hard with fear, taking her counsel on how to hunker down for the "doomsday period" on the 25th day of the month. When it came time for my period, I was as afraid as a camper running from a grizzly bear. I didn't know I had a serious case of FOMP—Fear Of My Periods. It was subtle. But I was gripped with fear each month. How could I be afraid of this normal part of being a woman, which I've had since fourteen? It was like being afraid of speaking in public or afraid of dark alleys and scary basements. It was real.

Then one day my friendship with Fear took a drastic turn. Her true colors came out. She was no longer seen as a concerned friend looking out for my well-being. She was aggressive, controlling and tormenting. That's when I realized all this time SHE WAS FAKING. Her manipulative speech was affecting me in a dangerous way. I had to acknowledge she wasn't my friend anymore. The friendship was unhealthy and not beneficial for me, and it had to end.

The first step was to acknowledge I had FOMP and that I wasn't resting in God's love. My period shouldn't be a fearful thing. Fear didn't come from God. He didn't want me to be fearful every month.

The second step was to confess the fear to God, my husband, and friends to bring it to the light. I need to trust in God's love for me and that He made my body wonderfully. I need a sound mind before and during my period. I need peace to cover my anxious thoughts each month. He created my period, and He is the God of my body.

Are you experiencing FOMP: Fear Of My Period syndrome or any other fear? If so, I want to encourage you not to listen to fear. Don't give it any attention. It's not a good friend, but a liar.

Yes, the symptoms are real. But living in fear of our periods or anything else is not our portion as children of God. God wants His daughters living in freedom, secure in His love, having sound minds (i.e. thoughts) and walking in power. His banner over you is perfect love,[8] and His love un-friends fear.

My Friend Named Fear

Here's what I'm asking God...

God, I confess the fear of my period and fear of any kind (of harm, danger, loss, rejection, failure, success, man, etc.). Lord, surround me with Your love; perfect me in your love. As I rest in your perfect love, it will cast out all forms of fear. Free me from the torment of anxious words and thoughts, and give me peace and a sound mind. Help me to think on those things that are true, lovely, noble, pure, just and of good report. (Philippians 4:8). I declare fear has no place in my life, heart, mind or soul.

Here's something to think on...

True love doesn't torment. And evil talk, whether from the outside or the inside corrupts even the best person. (1 John 4:18; 1 Corinthians 15:33).

Here's a tip to help you stand...

Un-friend fear: Speak the truth (i.e. God's word) in the face of fear's lies. Confess your FOMP to God, a trusted relative, a friend, or a spiritual leader who will pray for you. Get it out in the light. Understand that it's lying to you and can't tell the truth.

LETTER 8

Thorn in My Flesh

> "Beauty and thorns dwell side by side in the same place.
> Both are needed to make a beautiful scent and story."
> ~Chavos B.

Dear *Woman*,

Have you ever gotten a splinter in your finger? If so, you know it can be annoying. Recently, when I was packing to go home from a women's retreat, I got a splinter in my nail bed. It felt like someone was driving a needle in my skin. I tried to get it out, but I couldn't get all of it out by myself. I needed help. Holding out the middle finger on my left hand, I asked one of my friends, "Can you help me get this splinter out?"

She grabbed my finger to inspect it. "Hold on; let me get my glasses." Long pause. "Girl, how did you get the splinter under your nail bed?"

"I was picking up my shoe and scraped the floor with my nail. I got some of it out, but I need help with the rest." I was still holding out my throbbing finger like it was infected.

"Okay, let me get some tweezers," she said in a motherly tone.

My friend tried and tried and more came out. However, the more she tried the more it pushed down into my nail bed. My now, former friend was digging her way to China by way of my nail bed.

"I'm going to stop," she said, "because I'm too afraid I will push it further into your nail bed. O—kay, hon—ey. See if your husband can get it out for you when you get home."

I took my friend's advice and asked my beloved husband, "Can you get this stupid splinter out of my finger?" I was afraid I was going to get an infection. I'd had that splinter under my nail bed for a day and a half. It was red and puffy-looking and very tender.

"Yep, let me get a needle," he said, a little too excited to stick his wife with a sharp object.

I held out my finger, and closed my eyes so I wouldn't see the needle. He took my swollen finger and jabbed the needle under my nail to dig out the splinter. He tried and tried, relentless. He was not going to let that tiny sliver of wood defeat his manly self. My finger was now a round red pin cushion of flesh.

"Lover, it's okay. It hurts. Never mind, babe," I pleaded. He pulled pieces of it out, drawing a milk jar of blood.

"No, I can get it out."

The flesh around the nail looked like a peeled grapefruit, but he got the splinter out. It took three tries to get it out. What if try after try it didn't come out? I would still have that stupid splinter in my finger.

The apostle Paul had more than just a stupid splinter in his finger. He had a thorn in his flesh, which he doesn't give any detailed information about. We don't know if the thorn in his flesh was a sickness, a mental issue, a wound or something else. All we know is, he was given a thorn in his flesh to keep him humble. He wrote:

> "And lest I should be exalted above measure by the abundance of the revelations, a thorn in the flesh was given to me, a messenger of Satan to buffet me, lest I be exalted above measure."
> (2 Corinthians 12:7).

Paul asked God about his thorn three times and got no reprieve, no change and no removal of the thorn. Why didn't God remove it? I know He's not hard of hearing because there are accounts of God talking with Paul many times.[9] But this one request He didn't answer for Paul. Paul was all right with it and resolved to boast in his weakness.[10]

I've felt like I had a thorn in my flesh. A big fat splinter in my womb, called endometriosis. I've prayed and prayed for it to leave, and people have prayed and laid hands on me for it to leave. It doesn't want to leave. So, it must be a thorn right? Some would probably say, "No, your sickness is not a thorn in your flesh compared to Paul."

I agree, they're probably right.

I wasn't given divine inspiration to write half of the New Testament. I haven't been shipwrecked or persecuted. I'm not a Hebrew of Hebrews, from the tribe of Benjamin. I'm not a member of the Pharisees. I'm not called to be an apostle by God, and I didn't receive an abundance of revelations. I don't even try to compare myself to Paul. But I know what I experience in my life and body each month, so let's just say, it's a splinter compared to Paul's thorn.

This is no little splinter in my finger like the one my husband helped me with. This is bigger. The splinter (endo) in my flesh (aka womb) has been painful, uncomfortable, causing all sorts of problems and most of all, very humbling. It has humbled me and produced a level of brokenness and tenderness in my life like I've never had before. It has caused me to have compassion toward people suffering with an illness.

Do you feel you have a thorn (or a splinter) in your life? Have you prayed and prayed, changed your diet, exercised regularly doing your yoga, Pilates or running? And it still doesn't want to leave?

Be encouraged. There is glory and beauty in the midst of having thorns and being in thorny situations. You don't believe me? Look at roses. We ladies love roses, don't we? They come in all colors (pink, yellow, orange, purple, white) for all different occasions.

A rose is such a gorgeous flower, but when you look closer you will see the sticky, ugly, painful thorns coming from out of the stems. I love the rose, but the thorns—not so much. I can't enjoy the roses and at the same time reject the thorns, which are a part of this beautiful flower. Ah, beauty and thorns side by side in the same place. So it is, in my life and yours. We are beautiful roses among thorns. Let's embrace the thorns or splinters along with the beauty, expecting a greater glory that will be revealed in us in the end.

Here's what I'm asking God...

God, right now it's difficult for me to boast in my infirmities and embrace thorny situations. Let me see my life, issues, and situations the way you see them. Help me to follow Paul's example and boast in my infirmities. I declare God will give me beauty for ashes and the oil of joy for mourning.

Here's something to think on...

Jesus had a crown of thorns, but one day He will receive many crowns not made of thorns but of precious jewels. Paul had an abundance of revelation but only boasted in his infirmities. (2 Corinthians 12:9; Revelation 19:12).

Here's a tip to help you stand...

Receive the beauty and the thorns. Buy yourself a rose and observe it (What do you see? What about the thorns? What do they do?)

LETTER 9

Paralyzed By Endo

"Therefore strengthen the hands which hang down, and the feeble knees..."
~(Hebrews 12:12).

Dear *Woman*,

    I'm crippled. But I can walk. Though I have the ability to move my legs, I'm crippled on the inside. Endo caused so much agony, it looked like I was paying homage to the floor as I walked to the bathroom. As you know, the pain, cramps and heavy bleeding cripples you, leaving you feeling helpless. If people were to look at you and me on our good days, they wouldn't think we were dealing with a crippling disease. They would probably say, "If you hadn't told me, I would've never known you were struggling with this."

    The reason they can't tell is because, no matter what, we keep going and pressing through the crippling symptoms. Still believing, still reaching, still hoping, still dreaming and at times laughing while other times crying.

    You give encouragement and pray for others. You speak comforting words to women who need to be comforted. You give a helping hand and a listening ear. You serve and take care of your family and others unselfishly. You are a social activist causing positive change in your community. I admire you.

    There was this guy named Mephibosheth. (Don't try to say his name too fast). He was crippled and "lame in his feet." (See 2 Samuel 9). His daddy was Jonathan, the best friend of King David. One day, King David inquired about Saul's descendants. He wanted to show kindness to them for his friend,

Jonathan's sake. David found Mephibosheth and sent for him. I imagine Mephibosheth felt abandoned, rejected and all alone. He probably thought no one remembered or cared about a little ol' lame guy like him. And right then, there was a knock, and a note slid under the door. It had the royal signet seal on it. He broke the seal and opened it. The note read: "King David requests your presence at his table."

Wow, an invitation to the King's table. Can you hear Mephibosheth singing this song (performed by Tamela Mann) on his way to see the King?

> *"Take me to the King*
> *I don't have much to bring*
> *My heart is torn in pieces*
> *It's my offering.*
>
> *Lay me at the throne*
> *Leave me there alone*
> *To gaze upon Your glory*
> *Take me to the King."* [11]

Mephibosheth fell on his face and prostrated himself before King David. He gained favor with King David, and the king showed him kindness. He restored to Mephibosheth the land of his grandfather (inheritance) and invited him to eat bread at his table continually. [12]

You are *invited* to sit at the King's table. You have favor with the King of kings, and His favor is upon you like dew on the grass. There is a special place setting with your name on it. Don't worry about trying to muster up the strength to go. He will carry you like a shepherd whose sheep have been tired, weary, injured or whose legs were broken, and He will escort you to His banqueting table. He loves you. God, who is the King of Heaven will show kindness to you and lavish you with his extravagant love, mercy, gifts and provisions.

Bow down in worship before the Lord's throne. Eat from the King's table continually and enjoy the wine (intimacy of the Holy Spirit) and bread of life (His word). For in His presence there is fullness of joy, and at His right hand there are pleasures forever more.[13] This crippling disease can't stand up to the favor and kindness of God on your life. He will *strengthen* our feeble knees.

Here's what I'm asking God...

God, let your favor be upon me like dew upon the grass. Show me your loving-kindness each day. You are the Good Shepherd, who carries me through this life's journey. I recline at Your table and enjoy Your presence. I declare I will be strong in the Lord and in the power of His might. (Ephesians 6:10).

Here's something to think on...

"The lame will leap like a deer..." God specializes in healing the lame and strengthening feeble knees. (Isaiah 35:6*a*).

Here's a tip to help you stand...

Put on your favorite song and have a dance break—leap and dance for five minutes.

II. Eighteen Years

LETTER 10

Discouraged Avenue

"This is my command—be strong and courageous! Do not be afraid or discouraged. For the Lord your God is with you wherever you go."
~Joshua (Joshua 1:8 NLT).

Dear *Woman*,

I sat anxiously on the tan patient bed, swinging my feet back and forth and rubbing my hands together. I whispered to my husband, "I think I can hear Dr. Jones in the next room." We could hear muffled voices coming from next door as he spoke with a patient. Even though he was right next door, it was a while before he came through the door. We patiently waited as the time went by. Five minutes passed. Ten minutes passed. Fifteen minutes passed. After twenty minutes, our anxiety grew. My husband turned into a tap dancer before my eyes. He looked at the door and then at the time on his cell phone and up at me.

"I wonder when he will be done." I sounded frustrated.

This was how my surgery follow-up appointment began. After twenty-five minutes, he came swiftly through the door.

"Hello," said Dr. Jones. He had a manila folder in his hand.

"Hello, Dr. Jones," I said with anxiety in my voice.

"Hello, Sir," he said, while shaking my husband's hand and then mine.

"Well, let's have a look at some pictures from your surgery."

He pulled up his swivel stool right in front of me and fixed his glasses on his face. He said, "Has anyone ever told you that you have endometriosis?"

"Yes." I was confused by his question because I was the one who told him I had endometriosis at our first consultation.

"That you have stage four?" Dr. Jones pulled out pictures from my surgery.

"No!" I knew I had endo, but I didn't know it was that bad. I felt very concerned and alarmed by this new info.

"This is where the endometriosis was," he said, pointing at the pictures and circling the previous endo areas. "And here is the big endometrium mass that was on your left side."

"Hmmmm…"

"Yeah, it was a mess, really nasty in there," he said. "We went in and cleaned you all out." He flipped to the next picture.

"You still have some endometriosis here," he said, again circling a dark spot on the picture. "But the Lupron should take care of the rest. You had a hole here on your right side. It looks like maybe the endo ate through your wall."

Now I was afraid. Endometriosis eats, too.

Flipping to post-surgery cleanup shots, he said, "Surprisingly, your tubes are open on your right side and the fingers look good. The left side is not so good. I'm not sure if the fingers will work due to the damage from the endometriosis."

I sat there on the cold patient bed, and I glanced over at my husband with uncertainty in my eyes. I searched for some reaction in my husband's face to what the doctor told me. I took a deep breath like I was about to blow up a balloon. To be told my left fallopian tube isn't good felt like someone was attacking my womanhood and had just called me the "b word."

Dr. Jones stood up to throw something in the trash, leaned against the window and folded his arms. "Here is what I think. I think IVF is the best way. Your egg count is low, so you will have 30% chance with IVF. To succeed your egg level has to be above 0.5 ng/ml, and you're at 0.16 ng/ml." He spoke very matter-of-factly, with no hope at all.

I tried to process what the doctor was telling me, but it was so hard to hear his report. Water tried to flood my eyes, but I fought back the dam of tears from breaking out. No doctor had ever told me there was a small chance of becoming pregnant. I always had hoped that it would just happen. Now it seemed that hope was being snatched from my heart. All I heard was, "You can't produce a thing. Your eggs are bad. Good luck getting pregnant. And guess what, you have endometriosis at the worst level possible. Take that."

I didn't expect to receive that kind of news when I walked into the hospital that day. I had entered my appointment encouraged. I was hopeful after surgery and excited about the chance of the endo being gone, and shortly after that getting pregnant.

However, after my follow-up meeting, I was headed down "Discouraged Avenue" with each piece of information and every comment he spoke. I had to remember the good part, too, which was that the endo hadn't damaged my bowels, and the right fallopian tube looked okay. This part was drowned out by all the other news, so much so, that I couldn't even be happy about that part.

"We will do another follow-up," Dr. Jones said, looking down at my chart. "You're getting a shot each month of the Lupron Depot correct?"

"Yes," I replied.

"Okay, at the end of the twelve weeks, we will do another test to check your egg level, and then we can go from there."

Twelve weeks, there goes my hope of pregnancy for the new year.

"Okay." My heart sank like a deflated balloon.

I jumped up from the table with a look of despair and great concern on my face, walking out of the door with eyes to the floor. Dr. Jones reached over and patted me on my back. "It will be okay. You're okay."

The last thing my doctor said to me, after he told me the worst report ever, was prophetic and encouraging. He said, "It will be okay. You're okay." I believe God (The Creator) was speaking through the doctor that day. And He is speaking that over you, "It's going to be okay. You're okay."

After experiencing trouble and tragedy, David encouraged himself. You are an encourager, and you make a habit of encouraging people around you everyday. Now, it's time to take that gift of encouragement and encourage yourself. It's not selfishness at all. You need it. If it were a friend in need, you would encourage them without giving it a second thought. Go ahead and encourage yourself.

Here's what I'm asking God...

God, I'm discouraged. My soul is cast down, and my spirit is disquieted within me. It feels like my soul has gone to the grave. Bring encouragement to my soul, and give me a merry heart. Let the light of Your countenance be upon me and give me peace. You are my help and song. I declare I will arise and encourage myself in the Lord.

Here's something to think on...

God is working things out for your good. He is the help of your countenance. (Psalm 16:10, 43:5; Job 33:28-30).

Here's a tip to help you stand...

Encourage yourself: write a letter or declaration, draw a picture or do whatever you think will encourage you. Just encourage yourself, and tuck it away to read later when you need it, or post it up in a place where you can easily access it.

LETTER 11

Childbearing Years

"And now, Lord, what do I wait for? My hope is in You."
~David (Psalm 39:7).

Dear *Woman*,

The thought of having children has never gone away. Even after ten years of marriage, the desire hasn't gone away. You'd think by now it would've gone away. I never thought infertility would've been a problem for us. I figured when the time came for us to "start a family," it would happen without any problems or difficulty. It hasn't been like that at all. It's been a battle, a struggle and a long wait.

As I wait, the clock keeps ticking. The stats keep yelling in my ear: "Women at the age of 35 have a small chance of pregnancy…blah blah blah." This statement isn't comforting at all, as I will turn another year older soon. As I wait, my friends have had not only one child, but two or three. As I wait, my eggs get older, and I wonder if it will ever happen.

To face the fact that I'm infertile was very hard for me. To be told by the doctor that I have a 30% chance of getting pregnant was devastating to hear. Then to realize that I wasn't the only one in this situation was sad.

According to the American Society for Reproductive Medicine (ASRM): "30% to 50% of infertile women have endometriosis." [14] And the 2006-2010 National Survey of Family Growth stated: "11% of women (6.7 million) between the ages of 15-44 had impaired fecundity or difficulties conceiving or bringing a pregnancy to term. 1.5 million women between the ages of 15-44 dealt with infertility in the US.[15] These statistics are alarming and hard for me to read.

Maybe you're reading this, and you've had kids and want more, but are unable due to infertility. Or you've never been pregnant before, and can't be due to infertility. Maybe you've been pregnant and had a miscarriage due to infertility. Or maybe you're going through IVF, IUI, or some other fertility treatment. Maybe you're a young woman wanting to have kids when you get married, and you're wondering if you will be able to because of endo. Wherever you find yourself today, you're not alone. I'm not alone, even though I think I am at times. I might be the only one in my circle of friends going through this, but there are women out there—you, who understand what I'm going through. We're not alone.

I have hope that one day I will have a family. I don't know when, but there is a chance of hope. *Hope* is big. If I can hope, then there is a chance for something good to happen. I've wavered and thought it will never happen. I gave up hope a time or two, or three. Then I would hear stories from women (some of my close friends) who hoped for a child, and it happened for them. And I would read stories from the Bible of women like Sarah, Hannah, Rachel, and Elizabeth, and it would encourage me. Hope was restored in me.

I like Sarah's story. I take comfort in knowing that Sarah was well past her childbearing years, and she laughed when she was told she would have a son. (See Genesis 18).

Can you imagine Sarah hoping she'd get pregnant, and by age 35 nothing happened? It came and went. She hoped at 40, and nothing happened. She hoped at 50, and nothing happened. She hoped at 80, and nothing happened. I wonder if she lost hope along the way. Maybe she laughed because it was hard for her to believe she would get pregnant. I would've laughed, too. Then finally at age 90, something happened. She conceived a child. She got what she'd hoped for.

She probably heard throughout those years of waiting, "You will never get pregnant."

Or "Just keep believing. It will happen."

"Sarah, have you thought about adoption?"

The midwives probably told her, "Girl, you have a small chance of getting pregnant. Your egg level is about dried up."

Or "It will never happen; just accept it as God's will." At some point she might've believed it. I know I have, and I'm only 36. Then at the point when hope was about to be gone, an angel came and said to her husband, "...this time next year, and Sarah your wife will have a son."[16]

Sarah laughed, "Ha, ha, who, me, this old girl? Me, pregnant, at my age? I'm well beyond childbearing years." (Paraphrased)

God proved her wrong. All her hope over the years compounded and came to fullness at age 90.

I want to encourage you; don't give up hope today. I know hope deferred will make a heart sick. I've suffered from "hope deferred" many times. Then I'd hope again. Will you hope again? Hope for that childhood dream to come true. Hope for that long-awaited promotion. Hope for the restoration of a marriage relationship. Hope for the return of a prodigal child to come home. Hope for a friend's healing. Hope for the adoption to go through this time. Hope for the dream to be married one day. Hope for the dream to have another child. Hope for your first child. Hope for a healthy pregnancy this time. Hope for the possibility of a family when you get married. Hope for financial freedom. Hope for healing in your body. Hope. What is your dream? What is the desire of your heart? What was promised to you? Will you dare to hope again? If it doesn't happen today, then hope again tomorrow, but don't give up on hope.

Here's what I'm asking God...

God, I have suffered from hope deferred many times along this journey, which has caused my heart to be sick. Heal my heart and soul from hope deferred, and let the desire and dream that is in my heart come to pass. Let it be a tree of life to me. Restore my hope. I want to hope again. Anoint my eyes to see with hope glasses. I put my hope in You, for You are my hope. I declare I will hope again, and hope doesn't disappoint. (Romans 5:5).

Here's something to think on...

Hope wears invisible glasses and sees the future through them. (Hebrews 11:1).

Here's a tip to help you stand...

Spell out HOPE and create a cool acronym for the word. Here is mine:
> *Having*
> *Overcoming*
> *Peace*
> *Everlasting*

LETTER 12

Doctor, Doctor

"The things which are impossible with men are possible with God."
~Jesus (Luke 18:27).

Dear *Woman*,

I have an issue. An issue of blood. I've been to doctor after doctor, searching for answers about my issue. And seeking help and relief from my issue. I feel like singing, "Doctor, Doctor, don't tell me the news, I have a bad case of endo."

How many doctors have you been to for endo or your issue? I hope you've found one that knows how to help you. Hopefully, you didn't have to go to multiple doctors to get help like this lady in the Bible. (See Mark 5:25-34).

The Bible doesn't give the name of this lady, but it tells us that she had an issue of blood for twelve long years. She suffered greatly. She spent all of her life savings to fix her issue. She went to doctor after doctor, and instead of her issue getting better, it got worse. She tried everything, but nothing worked. She didn't find any relief from her issue until she touched the hem of Jesus's garment. When she touched Him, her issue immediately dried up.

He said to her, "Woman, your faith has made you whole."

All her searching and going from doctor to doctor was over.

The search for answers, trying to find relief can be wearisome, frustrating and tiring at times. But this lady pushed and persevered through the crowd of people despite her issue. She was determined to get her issue resolved.

Are you a woman with issues like me? What is your issue? Is it an issue of blood? An issue of pain? An issue of cramps? An issue of shame? An issue of sickness? An issue of depression? An issue of disappointment? An issue of hurt? An issue of rejection? An issue of envy? An issue of competition? An issue of unforgiveness? An issue of offense? An issue of doubt? An issue of fear? An issue of loneliness? An issue of insecurity? Despite our issues, let's press forward.

I know, you're determined not to let distractions, hindrances or roadblocks stop you from getting your issues resolved, from being whole and fulfilling your purpose and destiny. You have work to do. A business to run. Clothes to make. A cake to bake. Hair to style. Teeth to clean. Diapers to change. Classes to teach. Classes to take. Papers to write. Animals to nurture. Papers to grade. A game to play. A picture to draw. A seminar to teach. A movement to lead. People to coach. A speech to give. Or if you're like me, a book to write. No matter what it is, there is work to do.

So, we will persevere and push through in the midst of our issues to reach Jesus, the Doctor of all doctors, who knows exactly how to deal with our issues. He knows the right prescription that will work for us. There is no guesswork or practice with him. We can trust His prescription is the best for us; it won't make us worse, but better. And the Great Physician will speak over us: "Daughter, be of good comfort, your faith has made you whole."

Doctor, Doctor

Here's what I'm asking God...

God, thank you for physicians and medication, but You are the Great Physician, who has healing in Your wings. Although we go to physicians, and they prescribe medication for us, we put our trust and faith in You, not the doctors or the medicine. Direct my steps to find good doctors who can help, not harm. I am a woman with issues, and I bring them to You. Turn and use my issues for Your glory. Doctors have tried their best and come up short, but You never fail and never miss the mark. Will you perfect and complete that which concerns me? Make me whole. I declare I will be of good cheer, and my faith will make me whole.

Here's something to think on...

Faith heals. (Matthew 9:22).

Here's a tip to help you stand...

Prescription: Take two doses of faith, three times a day for the next seven days. Tell Dr. Jesus all about it. Write down your issues on a sheet of paper or in your journal.

LETTER 13

It's All in Your Head

"When Jesus saw him (Nathaniel) coming, he (Jesus) said, "There's a real Israelite, not a false bone in his body."
~John (John 1:47 MSG).

Dear *Woman*,

"It's all in your head. You are dwelling on it too much. It's all in your mind," my beloved husband said to me.

At first, he was ignorant about my disease. He had no clue. No understanding. After a conversation with his dad, my husband's attitude changed, and I am so grateful to my father-in-love.

Have you ever been told this? Shhh...don't say any names. You and I aren't the only ones to hear this popular phrase used often by people because they can't explain what is going on with us. They reduce it to our brain power.

They think the pain and all the symptoms we experience day after day with endo are somehow in our heads. Really? It can't be all in our heads. There are 176 million plus women experiencing the same thing all across the globe. How can this be all in our minds? They don't understand this invisible disease, and I can't blame them for it. I barely understand it. It is different from most visible diseases.

How do we explain to our loved ones, friends, co-workers and society about this disease when they can't see our pain or bloating or feel our horrible cramps, fatigue and the ocean waves in our stomachs? Well, those that live with us can see us bent over the toilet or balled up in the fetal position on the bed. And they can see all of that, and still say, "It's all in your head."

I imagine the woman with the twelve-year-long battle with an issue of blood dealing with people, who thought she was faking or overacting. "Girl, there's nothing wrong with you! Stop being so dramatic. You better quit faking. It's all in your head."

She didn't listen to them. She knew what she was experiencing was real. She knew it wasn't normal. She knew it wasn't all in her head. She felt it in her body. She heard about someone that could heal her, and she pressed on to see Him in spite of what others said. I encourage you to keep pressing through, too.

I don't care what you've been told. It's not all in your head. Don't believe them. It's hurtful to have close family members or friends say these things and think in the backs of their minds, "She's faking it." Why would anyone want to fake being in pain and agony? Fake vomiting. Fake diarrhea. Fake fatigue. Fake not wanting to go to a long-awaited event that was planned months ago. Fake taking off from work or missing school. I understand people can fake it. But not you and not me. What do we have to gain? We're not fakers or liars. There is no falsehood in you. You are the real deal.

I heard *"it's all in your head"* so often, I started to think, "Hey, maybe it really is all in my head." I tried to bring my thoughts under control. You know, take them captive. But I would still vomit, still have pain and still be extremely tired. The endo symptoms were still there. It was real. Not just in my head. What I experience each month is real.

It's real for you, too. You know what you feel is real. Real pain. Real cramps. Real nausea. Real fatigue. Real time off work or school. Real disappointment from missing important events you had on your calendar for months.

Be encouraged; you have sisters around the globe going through the same thing, and they believe you. I believe you. And for those who don't believe us let's extend grace to them and forgive them for the words spoken out of their ignorance because they have no clue what we go through.

David said, "My loved ones and my friends stand aloof from my plague." (Psalm 38:11). We must pray for them to gain knowledge and understanding about this chronic disease.

We will take the stand, and lift our right hands up and put our left hands on the Bible, and say, "We promise, to tell the truth, the whole truth and nothing but the truth, so help us God."

Here's what I'm asking God...

God, you see my heart and know that I've spoken the truth. You desire truth in my inward parts. People have thought and said that I was faking, overacting and lying. God, this hurts. Heal my heart from all false statements. Defend me, O Lord, against those who have spoken falsely against me, and reveal the truth of my situation to them. I declare I am righteous in your eyes, and I don't have to prove myself to anyone, for You see me and know me.

Here's something to think on...

He will vindicate you. God knows you haven't sworn to falsehood, and he knows your integrity. (Psalm 24:4, 26:1).

Here's a tip to help you stand...

Forgive, extend mercy, and bless those who don't have a clue what you go through.

LETTER 14

The Waiting Room

"Patience is not just about waiting for something...
It's about how you wait or your attitude while waiting." [17]

~Joyce Meyer

Dear *Woman*,

I'm a little impatient when it comes to waiting. Waiting is part of our life, isn't it? Waiting in line at the grocery store or in the fast-food line to order food. Waiting in line to renew a driver's license or pay a bill. Waiting in line for a concert or amusement park ride. Waiting at the bus-stop for the bus to come. Waiting at the intersection for the light to turn green.

How about sitting in a waiting room? This is the worst. Waiting for your name to be called as you wait to see the doctor, or your banker or counselor. Sitting with your gaze locked on the entry door to the back or the front desk just waiting for someone to call your name or say those eight powerful words, "I can help whoever is next in line."

We quickly jump to our feet and dash to the door as if trying to beat someone with the same name. Or as if someone was going to jump ahead of us in line. We can't escape waiting. It's everywhere. Waiting can be so tiring. It wears us down.

There is a saying, "Good things come to those who wait." It's true. It's not easy, but in the end it was worth the wait. Waiting builds perseverance, character and that famous p-word "patience" in us, doesn't it. Can you testify to this? I appreciate things that I had to wait a little while for. It meant more and had a greater value than if I would've gotten it when I wanted it.

The waiting process shines light and reveals things in my heart: impatience, jealousy and wrong attitudes like: "How come they got called before me?" or "How come they got that before I did?" or "I was here first." It exposes my complaining and murmuring spirit. Have you ever said any of the following to yourself? "What's taking them so long? What's taking God so long? I should've been called by now. I should've had this or that by now. It doesn't take that long to do that."

The waiting process also shines light on my attitude of wanting it quickly, wanting it now, wanting it yesterday. I like to call it the "microwave-age" mindset. Or the drive-thru, have-it-my-way, faster-is-better age.

People hate to wait anymore. At the store, I've seen impatient people leave their stuff in the cashier line. It wasn't quick enough. Grocers created self-checkout stations because people hate to wait in line. What's next? Self-checkout at the doctor's office?

I want to be a more patient waiter. I need the *grace to wait* and a heart of humility to not feel like what I'm waiting on is entitled to me. I want to *wait with gladness* for others whose turn is now, and be at peace that my turn is coming up soon. I want to have a waiting posture like David, who is a good example of how to wait. He said: "My soul, wait silently for God alone, for my expectation is from Him. I wait for the Lord, my soul waits, and in His word I do hope." (Psalm 62:5, 130:5).

Why are you in the waiting room? Are you waiting on your healing? Waiting on a new job opportunity or new career? Waiting on clarity and direction? Waiting on promises to be fulfilled? Waiting on restoration and reconciliation with a family member? Waiting on a much-needed promotion? Waiting on a publishing contract? Waiting on the adoption process? What are you waiting on? *Your waiting will not be in vain.*

As you are in the waiting room, things are being prepared for you. Relax and sit back, rest, take a nap. Read a nice book as you wait. Complete an unfinished project. Make a new friend. You can have joy in the wait. In the waiting room, anticipation builds. *You're becoming stronger,* as you wait on the Lord. Your turn will be next. You will hear, "I can help whoever is next in line."

Here's what I'm asking God...

God, I wait on You. Let my waiting posture and attitude be like David, one of peace, gratefulness, patience, joy, satisfaction and contentment. I admit I've become impatient during the wait, and want "it" fast and now. The times, months and years seem to go by slowly as I wait on You to give me what I've been asking for. I believe You know when the time is right and best for me. Help me not get caught-up in the time, but trust that *my times* are in Your hands.

Here's something to think on...

Your strength is renewed as you wait. (Psalm 27:14; Isaiah 40:31).

Here's a tip to help you stand...

Waiting assessment: Take a self-examination/survey next time you're in a waiting room or line (use the regular line instead of the express). Are you a good waiter? Rate yourself on a scale of 1 to 10, with 1 meaning "No, I hate to wait" and 10 meaning "Yes, I love to wait." Take note of your attitude, reactions, and feelings and watch others' reactions and attitudes as they wait.

Bad Reports

"The light of the eyes rejoices the heart, and a good report makes the bones healthy."
~King Solomon (Proverbs 15:30).

Dear *Woman*,

I've been told I look like a train wreck. Mean, huh? I know. It wasn't about my outward appearance, but about my insides, like that makes it any better.

As I lay on the table, looking over at the black-and-white images on the sonogram screen, I asked the nurse technician, "What do you see?"

"It looks like you have a mass right here in the middle-left of your uterus." She circled a dark spot on the screen with her finger.

"Oh, o-kay. Do you see anything on my right side? I've had pain and a pulling feeling there from time to time." This had been going on for about a year.

Moving the sonogram stick to the right side. She said, "Let me check."

I squirmed a little from the discomfort.

"No, I don't see anything on that side. Maybe the mass on your left is pushing things over to the right. I'll tell you what, you are a train wreck in here," she said nonchalantly.

I did not want to hear I was a train-wreck on the inside.

Why does it seem like the doctors never give good news? Well, I shouldn't say never...they give pregnancy announcements, which is good news. But depending on the situation I guess that announcement could be bad news. I would love to hear from a doctor at least once, "Every thing looks good. You are fine."

I don't like bad news. I dislike bad news so much so that I don't watch the news because 90% of it is bad reports. Bad news just rips into pieces any ounce of joy and peace in our lives, doesn't it?

I'm not against doctors and the news; they do have their place. It would be nice to see some hope mixed in when they give a report. That's all. It would've been a little bit nicer, if the nurse technician, would have said, "You look like a train wreck in there, but not for long. The doctor is going to fix you right up." I guess I shouldn't expect doctors to be motivational speakers or coaches.

The bad reports have come. Now what do I do, and what is my response? When the bad reports come, it takes me by surprise and causes an emotional earthquake, putting cracks in my hopes and dreams and trying to shake the foundation of faith in my heart. I've cried and questioned. And cried and questioned some more. Disappointed by the bad news I've received.

Have you received some bad news and been disappointed, too? Have you been given a bad report like "you look like a train wreck" or worse? That doctor's report of being told you have endometriosis (stage 4), or cancer and there is no cure? Or told you have Polycystic Ovary Syndrome (PCOS), you're infertile, have a heart disease, you have to get a hysterectomy, or a loved one died, or a spouse hasn't been faithful? Bad news that you're fired or laid off from a job you've been at for 20 plus years? The list of bad reports goes on and on.

Bad reports will continue to come from the news, from the doctors, from family members and other sources. But then I hear this Bible verse encouraging us,

> "Surely the righteous will never be shaken; they will be remembered forever. They will have *no fear of bad news*; their hearts are steadfast, trusting in the Lord." (Psalm 112:6-7 NIV).

The Lord gives *good reports*. His plans for us are good. His goodness follows us. We will taste and see that He is *good*. He will satisfy us with good things. He will not withhold *any good* thing from those that are upright.[18] His report is "No weapon formed against you will prosper" (Isaiah 54:17). His report is, "I will deliver you out of all your afflictions" (Psalm 34:19). His report is, "I'm a Healer, and I work miracles." The Lord comes with a good report over you and me.

My Granny always told me, "There's two sides to every story." I've heard some say, "There's three sides to every story." Whichever one, the point is, there is another view. Yes, there will be bad reports, but then there's another side—the *Lord's report*.

Here's what I'm asking God...

God, I've received bad news that has brought discouragement, disappointment, depression, emotional earthquakes and some shaking to my faith. It doesn't feel good to hear the bad reports. (Name the bad reports.) I want to walk by faith and not by what I see or the reports that I hear. Help me to see from Your perspective and believe Your report. I will taste and see that You, Lord are good. Will You crown the year with Your goodness? (Psalm 65:11). I declare the good news of Your word over every one of my bad reports.

Here's something to think on...

There is a Heavenly doctor who doesn't give any bad news. He came to bring good news. (Lamentations 3:25-26; Luke 4:18 NLT).

Here's a tip to help you stand...

Take a 3 x 5 index card and at the top of it, write "Bad Reports." Write down all the bad reports you've received. Then flip it over on the other side and at the top write "*Good Reports*." What's the good side? Write down all the good. If you can't think of anything, write the *good* you want to see.

LETTER 16

I'm a Barren Mess

"He grants the barren woman a home, like a joyful mother of children."
~David (Psalm 113:9).

Dear *Woman*,

I'm a barren mess. I felt like I couldn't produce anything (a child, a book, a business). It seemed like everyone around me was being fruitful and multiplying. And I wasn't. I haven't. When other people are in their fruitful season, it's lonely because I can't relate. During my *barren season*, I have received comfort from Hannah's story over and over again. (See 1 Samuel 1).

Hannah was a barren mess. She was married to a man, who had another wife named Peninnah. The fact that he had two wives is another story. But Elkanah loved him *some* Hannah. Elkanah gave Hannah a double portion because the Lord closed her womb. His other wife, Peninnah was popping children out left and right, year after year (paraphrased).

While, year after year, Hannah sat in her barren season desiring to be fruitful. Desiring to be pregnant. Desiring to be a mother. Peninnah taunted Hannah for not being able to have children, to the point where Hannah cried and refused to lift one piece of unleavened bread to her mouth to eat.

On top of being barren and taunted by her husband's other wife, Eli, the priest accused Hannah of being drunk at a prayer meeting. This story sounds like an old-century soap opera, huh. Can you believe the Bible has such juicy and scandalous stories?

Hannah addressed the whole drunk-at-the-prayer-meeting issue with Eli, the priest. She said, "No, my lord, I am a woman of sorrowful spirit. I have drunk neither wine nor intoxicating drink, but have poured out my soul before the Lord." (1 Samuel 1:15). And he blessed her prayer request. A year later, after that prayer meeting, Hannah became pregnant. She entered into a fruitful season.

Along this journey of almost ten years of being in a barren season, I've encountered the spirit of Peninnah, where the fruitfulness of others has taunted me. It came in the form of baby showers, baby announcements, and big bellies everywhere, which quickly changed into *babies* everywhere. Peninnah's taunts became louder during one particular time of my barren season.

We attended a church full of late 20s and 30s-something couples. It started out okay—there were a few Hannahs in the place waiting on the promise of a child, and I could relate to them and vice versa. I took comfort being among Hannahs. However, over time, the fruitful season came for those once-upon-a-time barren Hannahs.

One by one, they began popping out babies. And women who already had kids were popping out babies, too. Some of these women were my friends, who've waited a while for a child. I rejoiced with them. I was happy for them because we prayed for them, and our prayers were answered, but I was sad and disappointed, too because the fact remained that I was barren. A barren fig tree without fruit in the middle of harvest time (I think we were the only couple without kids in the church before we left). I stood out more and more, and you could easily recognize my barren-fig-tree life.

Those of you in the barren season like me know it can be a lonely place. But guess what? It's only a season. Depending on where you live, there are four seasons (spring, summer, fall and winter). Where I'm from, in Missouri, these seasons last for three months each. I have an expectation that the seasons will change, and my favorite season, spring, is just around the corner. Well, I expected this barren season to be three months, too. I realized it doesn't work like that in the life of human beings. It could take years.

I didn't always understand God's perfect will for this season, and I never saw the beauty of it until recently. I'm coming to better understand—there is beauty in barrenness. A barren, dry, wilderness season can yield beautiful things. I think about the winter season, when everything is dry, fruitless, dead and barren. However, when the snow flakes fall, they cover everything with a white sheet. It's so beautiful. I love to see fresh snow fall.

The *beautiful part of my barren season* has been a deep closeness, intimacy, communication, friendship, and understanding with my husband. I'm learning all I can about God and myself in this place, and looking for the beauty in this season. I trust, God will make all things (even my barrenness) beautiful in His time.

Are you in a barren season? In a dry wilderness place? Whether barren in the sense of unable to have kids or barren in the sense of being unable to work, be encouraged. If you're unable to create. Unable to invent. Unable to produce products or services. Unable to make new friends. Unable to get started. Be encouraged, God will make a *beautiful stream in your barren season.* Before you know it this season will be over; it will not last forever.

You remember barren Hannah. Her barren season ended, and she not only had a son but five more children. Look who's popping children out left and right now. Her season of fruitfulness finally came. So will yours. And mine. Why? Because we were created and commissioned to be fruitful, to multiply and have dominion in the earth.[19] I'm not just talking about children here, but being fruitful in your business. Fruitful in your relationships. Fruitful in your finances. Fruitful in your creativity. Fruitful in whatever way God has ordained for you to be.

May we be like a fruitful vine, and a *"tree planted by the rivers of water, that brings forth its fruit in its season, whose leaf also shall not wither; And whatever he does shall prosper."* (Psalm 1:3).

Here's what I'm asking God...

God, cause me to see the beauty in my barren season. You make all things beautiful in Your time. I fix my eyes on You and not on those around me that are in their fruitful season, let me not be taunted, sad, jealous or envious by their fruitful season. Rather, I choose to rejoice with them. I know this season will come to an end, and I will enter a season of abundance and fruitfulness. Give me the grace to endure and be content in every season of my life, understanding that this season will not last forever. I declare springtime is coming in my life, and the dead and dry things will come alive again. I will be fruitful in my season according to Psalm 1.

Here's something to think on...

God blesses the barren, and you're called to be fruitful.
(Genesis 1:28; Psalm 113:9).

Here's a tip to help you stand...

Sing in your barren season. Put on your favorite song and sing along to it. Or if you're feeling creative, make up your own song. It's time to *SING!*

LETTER 17

Why Have You Forsaken Me?

"I will never leave you nor forsake you."
~God (Hebrews 13:5).

Dear *Woman*,

I felt forsaken by God. I've read and often quoted the scripture in Hebrews 13:5, which says, "I will never leave you nor forsake you." I never thought that one day I wouldn't fully believe that God will never leave me nor forsake me.

It was December 2012, and it seemed like I had cried out to God numerous times about being healed from endo, and it was to the point where I was *done* again. I was tired of dealing with it month after month every year. A couple days before Aunt Flo's arrival, I came across a scripture in Psalm 33 where David said, "I cried out to the Lord, and he heard my cry and healed me." I loved this Psalm, so I prayed to God and cried out to Him like David did. I thought, "That was it. It's finished." I did what the scripture said, so now I am healed.

Not so fast. Instead of being healed and relieved from my symptoms, Aunt Flo's visit was worse than I'd experienced in previous months. It's like she heard my prayers for her to be better, and she was in rebellion and rage against it. I saw the inside of a plastic bag or toilet bowl five times during her visit that month.

"I'll teach you for praying against me." She sneered.

My prayers and cries went unanswered, and I started to believe God had forsaken me.

Standing at the sink one day trying to hold my thoughts and feelings in, I blurted out to my husband, "I feel like God has forsaken me." I slammed a plate into our silver dish tray. "I've prayed and prayed about this issue. I even did what David did in Psalm 33, and nothing happened."

My husband came and put his hand on my shoulder as I stood at the sink. He tried to encourage me during this time: "You know what the Bible says— 'God will never leave you nor forsake you,' Chavos."

I looked at him with disbelief, disdain and hurt in my eyes. I wanted to believe it, but it was a challenge for me when my feelings screamed louder than the truth. I snapped back with tears hitting my shirt, "Sure, yeah right. I know what the scriptures say, but it's difficult to believe that right now."

He lovingly said, "I know, but just because you don't believe it doesn't mean it's not true." He reached over to kiss my forehead.

"I know, but I can't. That's how I feel."

I was reminded about how Jesus felt forsaken by His Father while on the cross. He cried out to God, "Eli, Eli, lama sabachthani? My God, My God, why have You forsaken me?" (Matthew 27:46) I didn't feel too bad knowing that Jesus had shared these feelings, too.

I was in a very hard and dark place. I couldn't pray and really didn't want to, either. My attitude was: "Why pray, what's the point? God doesn't hear my prayers anyway."

In the back of my mind, I knew what I felt was contrary to what I knew to be true. I knew God answered prayer because I had experienced it, time and time again in the past. But I didn't believe it during this time. It felt like my prayers were going to the spam box—never to be opened.

This feeling of being forsaken lingered on for a week or two. Desperate to know if anyone else had ever felt like God had forsaken them, I searched: "forsaken by God" and found several articles that were very alarming, but encouraging. In summary, these articles explained how Satan is on a mission to destroy the person who feels forsaken and their prayer life because they stop believing God hears their prayers. These article should've had my name in it. They explained my state perfectly.

Why Have You Forsaken Me?

After I read that article, I knew I was in trouble spiritually. I knew I was in trouble mentally. I knew I was in trouble emotionally. The problem was I didn't know how to get out of the trouble. I didn't have it in me to fight, pray or quote scripture, so I reached out to one of my spiritual mothers.

With tears in my eyes, I typed:

Dear Deborah, I need your prayers... I feel like God has forsaken me, and I'm angry with Him. I have cried out for Him to heal me from endometriosis for eight years, and I feel like He hasn't heard my cry. I have been told that it's wrong to be angry with God, and I don't want to be. But it's hard for me to stay in faith when month after month the same thing happens with no real lasting change.

She emailed back within hours: I will fast for you and Garry tomorrow and agree with you that God will remove this oppression from the enemy. Lots of Love sent to you.

Wow, that's the Body of Christ. I was blown away by this act of love and selflessness. Never have I had anyone fast for me. Thank God for mentors. I was stirred by her email to set my mind to fast the next day, too. Over the course of several days, light began to break through the dark season of my soul, and I experienced breakthrough and freedom. I cried out to God again and told him how I felt forsaken and renounced the lies of the enemy. Healing of a different kind, not physical but emotional, took place during that time.

Maybe you are in the place where you have cried out to God over and over for the same issue and no answer. And you feel like God has forsaken you. I understand that feeling is very real and strong. So strong that it muffles the truth of God's promise that He would *never forsake us*. Jesus was forsaken on the cross, so that we would never be forsaken. He is near to you at this time, though you may feel He's far away. *He is there!*

Here's what I'm asking God...

God, bring comfort and healing to me in the midst of my pain and hurt. Let me know that You are near. You are not a liar, and Your promises are true, even though it's hard for me to see right now because of my circumstances. I've heard and read that You will never leave me nor forsake me. God, where are You? Draw near to me, and I will run to You. Jesus, thank You for comforting me. You understand my feeling forsaken, for You have felt forsaken before. Thank You for interceding for me. I renounce the lies that say, "You have abandoned and forsaken me." Let the truth of Your Word speak louder than my feelings and situations. I declare You are Immanuel. You are God with us.

Here's something to think on...

He (Immanuel) is with you and doesn't forsake those who seek Him. (Matthew 1:23; Psalm 9:10).

Here's a tip to help you stand...

Smother isolation and feeling forsaken by hanging out with a good friend and asking them for prayer.

LETTER 18

God, I'm Angry With You

> "'Be angry, and do not sin': do not let the sun
> go down on your wrath."
> ~Apostle Paul (Ephesians 4:26).

Dear *Woman*,

God came to visit me today like He does every day. He pulled up a chair and sat a while and listened to me as I spoke about my day, my desires, my hopes, my dreams and fears. I talked to Him about my husband, my family and my friends. He listened and leaned in closer with concern and love in His eyes. His ears were inclined to me. I had His attention. He waited patiently for His turn to speak.

I sang some of His favorite songs. I would lose my key, and my voice would sound like I was whining.

He didn't care though. He smiled. He loved to hear my weak worship to Him.

My favorite questions to ask Him are: "What is on Your heart? What is Your will?" I waited expectantly and eager to hear His response to me. At times He would be silent, staring at me, and other times, He would answer me.

This meeting would take place the same time every morning, on the third floor of my house, in my loft room with wall-to-wall, thick, soft light-blue carpet. He likes to meet early in the morning around 5:00. At times I'm so tired from the previous day's activities that I miss our meetings. But He is gracious to meet me when I wake up later around 6, 7, or 8.

I knew Aunt Flo's visit was near, so at one of my meetings with God, I dared to ask Him again: "God, please let Aunt Flo's visit be sweet, kind and pleasurable and no vomiting this time. Heal me from this horrible disease, and give me relief. It's in Your Son Jesus's name I pray."

After that prayer I was confident that He heard me, and it was the end of my horrible disease. Aunt Flo would be sweet, indeed.

Nope, she wasn't. Aunt Flo was sour. She was on a war-path to totally destroy me. It was the normal visit (vomiting, dehydration, pain, cramps, and heavy bleeding) but super-sized. My brown leather couch gave me comfort all day and night.

As I lay on my couch, thoughts entered my mind: "See, you prayed for your period to be better, and it wasn't. God didn't listen to you at all. You've met with Him everyday for years, and this one thing you ask, He ignores it." The words sunk down into my heart and lodged there for habitation. Those thoughts stayed there habitually resting and growing for days. I believed it.

The time for my regular meeting with God at 5:00 a.m. came and went. Then 6 came and went. God waited, desiring to meet with me wondering where I was. 7 a.m. came and went. 8 came and went. There was no meeting with God that day. The next day at 5, my eyes popped open. I lay looking up at my white textured ceiling. I knew what time it was. I didn't feel like talking to God. I rolled over on my side and covered my head with the brown comforter, and fell back to sleep. 6 came, and I ignored the call to talk to God again. This went on for several days, which turned into a couple of weeks.

My once-close meeting—where there was singing and conversation with God—ceased. The third floor was a distant place and not a desirable place for me at all. It reminded me that my prayers were banned from reaching Heaven, so why should I ascend the baby-blue carpeted flight of stairs to meet with God. The thought of talking to God about the same issue for years and no answer caused me to want to rip up that baby-blue carpet leading to the great upstairs, bolt the door shut, and nail a sign on it that says: "DO NOT ASCEND. NO PRAYERS ANSWERED HERE.

I don't understand. I have asked Him over and over. The Bible encourages me to keep asking, seeking and knocking.[20] And if I do, the door will be opened, I will find what I was looking for, and I will get what I asked for. Well, I asked and asked and didn't get it. I was tired of asking. I was done praying.

I knew eventually I would have to face God. When we finally met, our meeting wasn't in our normal place. This time it was in my tan Honda Accord in a parking lot. It was different scenery for us. Maybe it was needed because the normal place held hurt, disappointment and discouragement.

I sat in the car with thoughts swirling in my head about my issue and how my prayers weren't heard. That was a very soft spot for me. Tears began to fill my eyes like water filling a tub and overflowing onto my cheek, running down to my chin. My heart was trying to come out of my rib cage and onto my lap. I suddenly had a personal summer in the middle of the winter.

I was about to utter some words that were downright blasphemous in some religious arenas. I've been taught and warned never to say it or be this way to the Almighty God. So, it was hard for me to make my mouth speak it. God watched and waited and looked at me, knowing what I was about to utter to Him. It had already been a while since we'd spoken, and these were the first words I chose to say to Him. My heart was pounding. "God," I quivered.

"Yes, daughter." He responded with a tender voice.

"I'm angry with You. There I said it." I waited for a bolt of lightning to come through the roof of my car and strike me dead on the spot. It didn't. I'm still around to tell you about it.

The elephant that was sitting on my shoulders suddenly got up and strolled away. In that moment relief filled my soul. But then I soon felt guilty because I was taught not to be angry with God.

No matter the teaching, my confession that day opened up the door for God to heal my heart. My heart became more and more pliable and tender. The desire to meet with Him in our special place came dancing back into my soul and heart. After a week or two, I ventured the baby-blue steps to the great upstairs and met with God.

I'm not the first person, nor will I be the last, to voice being offended or angry with God. He didn't strike them or me down for being honest with Him. But if I examined myself and the situation, I really didn't have anything to be angry or offended about. I've accepted the American Santa Claus god—that if I do everything good, I will end up on His good list and get everything I asked for, when I asked for it and how I asked for it.

I've learned it doesn't work that way, not with God. It didn't work like that when I was a child. I didn't get everything I wanted as a child from my parents. Did you? So why would I think it would be like that with my Heavenly Father? Why would I think He would answer my every call? If we're honest, our anger and offense with Him comes because something we sought God for didn't happen, or something happened that we didn't expect.

If you've never been angry with God, that's good. If you are, don't feel guilty or scared as if He will strike you down for being angry or offended with Him. It is what we do with that offense and anger that matters. You can be angry, but don't sin per the Apostle Paul.

Confess it to God. He is *BIG* enough to handle His children being offended or upset with Him. He's not like people. People are fickle. If you told someone that you were angry with them, you telling them that may incite anger in them or they may be offended. But God is God enough to deal with it.

It doesn't matter if we sit with our arms crossed, with pout faces and hearts. He waits as a loving Father to meet with us. He's patient with us. He longs to be with us.

God, I'm Angry With You

Here's what I'm asking God...

God, I confess I am (or was) angry with you, and I don't want to be. But my situations, circumstances and symptoms speak to me and say, "You've prayed, but your prayers aren't heard. So, why trust or continue to pray." I have listened and believed. I haven't had a desire to seek Your face or to pray because of disappointments. I want to feel Your closeness again and have the relationship we once had.

Heal my emotions and broken heart from the disappointment of things that didn't happen or things that did happen that I felt shouldn't have. Give me grace to accept Your will and trust that You hear me when I pray, even without the answer. I declare the Lord hears the prayer of the righteous, and when they cry out to Him, He hears and delivers them out of all their troubles. (Psalm 34:17).

Here's something to think on...

The Lord is near to those who have a broken heart. (Psalm 34:18).

Here's a tip to help you stand...

Pull up a chair or lay on the floor and tell God all about it. He can handle it.

III. Could No Wise Lift Herself Up

LETTER 19

I'm So Weak

"Have mercy on me, O Lord, for I am weak..."
~David (Psalm 6:2).

Dear *Woman*,

During endo episodes, I'm reminded that I'm not so strong. My eyelids feel like weights are on them causing them to close, and there is a three-day stand off between my stomach and my food; my stomach wins every time. My brown lips dry up and turn white, looking like white frosted flakes (aka cracked), and my tongue and throat long for a nice cool water bath. My legs feel like they've dissolved into liquid. It takes everything in me to gather some strength to simply walk to the bathroom. I go bent over taking the dreaded walk to what awaits me.

I don't want to talk. It takes a lot of energy to move my mouth, but I know I need help. I open my cracked dry mouth and whisper, "God, I'm so weak please help me."

God said the same thing to me that He spoke to Apostle Paul, "Daughter, My strength is made perfect in your weakness."

Paul gained understanding and revelation of God's strength in his weakness that only would've come during his times of weakness. If he didn't have any weak moments, he wouldn't have experienced God's strength perfected in him.

God is *strong* in the midst of our weakest point. There were times when I was weak, but I felt the strength of God complete and mature in me. I don't fully understand how that works. I know it sounds backwards. I would think His strength would be made perfect in my strength, but why would I need the perfection of the strength of God when I'm strong. I need it the most when I'm weak. This is what I learned in my weak moments, which are more often these days.

How are you feeling today? Are you feeling weak? Tired? Fatigued? It's okay. Just rest and know, "He gives power to the weak and to those who have no might He increases strength." (Isaiah 40:29). He girds you with strength for the battle, and you can step on the neck of any disease, for by your God you can run through a troop and leap over every wall.[21] Whether it's a wall of sickness, a wall of despair, a wall of discouragement, a wall of fear or a wall of failure. Whatever the wall, He has given us the strength, power and ability with our weak selves to jump over it.

He speaks over you and me, "Arise, my daughter and strengthen that which is left (all that remains). *My strength* is being made perfect right now in you, right there in your weakness. Embrace the maturation process of My strength inside of you."

What a privilege we have to experience the strength of God complete and mature in us. I know it might not seem like a privilege right now. But trust me, we will see it in the end. He won't leave His strength undeveloped and immature in us. He who began a work in us is faithful to complete it.

The Lord your God in your midst is mighty to save.[22] The joy of the Lord is our strength.[23] He is the strong and mighty One able to uphold us in our weakness.

I'm So Weak

Here's what I'm asking God...

God, I'm weak and can't lift myself up. Let me see my weak moments as an opportunity for You to show Yourself strong in me. Let Your strength be complete, perfect and mature in me. Give me power and increase Your strength in me.

Here's something to think on...

Our weak moments allow God the opportunity to mature and show forth His strength in us. (2 Corinthians 12:9).

Here's a tip to help you stand...

See your weak moments as strength training by God. Lift some weights: Do 10 reps of "*Joy-bells.*"

LETTER 20

I Give Up

"If we endure hardship, we will reign with him (Jesus)."
~Apostle Paul (2 Timothy 2:12 NLT).

Dear *Woman*,

Whatever you do, don't give up. Not now. You have seen and experienced so much. There are people who look up to you. There are things you are yet to see and do. There are places to go and people to encourage. Books to be written. Songs to sing. Businesses to run. Classes to take and to teach. Husbands to feed. ☺ Kids to train. Orphans to visit. Marathons to run. Roads to travel.

If you give up now, people will miss out on what God put inside of you. They will miss out on your story of triumph, your testimony, your creativity, your impact, and your uniqueness. You're not a quitter. You still have some fight left in you. Just think, you've made it this far. You are relentless.

I wanted to give up several times, and I did. The battle with endo was wearing me down and kicking my butt. It was overwhelming and too big for me to handle. I lifted my hands with palms out as if endo said, "Freeze, turn around and put your hands in the air."

I didn't have the strength to fight one more month. I cried out, "Lord, I give up. I can't do this anymore."

That simple and honest prayer to the Lord opened the door for help from the Father. He comforted me, and I knew that help was on the way. I tried to battle in my own might, power and strength, and it didn't work. But when His strength, courage, help and determination came, I got a second wind to make it another day and another month. I mounted up like an eagle and flew high above my storm.

You and I were made to soar and to fly far above every storm like eagles. Don't give up, but *mount up!* Mount up in the strength of your God. Mount up in His power. Mount up in courage. Mount up, *Dear Woman*. For He gives His people strength. (See Isaiah 40:31). Let's get Heavenly altitude and see from a kingdom perspective. He's blowing the wind of the Spirit under you to cause you to glide. Let's catch the wind and soar.

Here's what I'm asking God...

God, cause me to be strong in You, Lord, and in the power of Your might. Be mighty in my midst. Make me steadfast, unmovable and relentless in the face of my circumstances. I can't walk this journey on my own. It's not by my might nor by my power, but by Your Spirit, Oh Lord, that I can run and not be weary, and I can walk and not faint. I declare: I will mount up on wings as an eagle and soar high above the storms with the Spirit as my wind.

Here's something to think on...

There's a harvest due and coming to those who don't give up. (Galatians 6:9).

Here's a tip to help you stand...

Take a flight on "Air Eagle." Research eagles. (What kind of eagle are you?) Color an eagle. Find one attribute you can identify with and make a poster board, key chain or bracelet as a token that you're like an eagle.

LETTER 21

Lord, Carest Thou Not?

"Casting all your care upon Him, for He cares for you."
~Peter (1 Peter 5:7).

Dear *Woman*,

The Lord doesn't care. At least that is what it felt like while in the midst of my storms. Have you felt like that? Does it feel like the Lord is unaware or that He even cares about you and what you are going through in your life or in your body? Does it appear He is off busy somewhere taking care of other people in the universe or asleep while you're in a storm?

Jesus's disciples felt like He didn't care about them, either. There was a great storm taking place in their lives, and Jesus was on board the boat (See Mark 4:35-41). But he was sound asleep at the bottom of the boat. The disciples ran to Jesus to tell Him about what was going on as if He didn't know.

They said, "Teacher, do You not care that we are perishing?"[24]

Imagine, Jesus's disciples feeling like the Lord didn't care. These guys walked and ate with Him daily. They were his boys. His boys, whom He sent out two by two into cities for ministry. His boys, whom He gave power over serpents and scorpions. His boys, whom He hand selected to teach and follow Him. These very men now felt like their teacher didn't care. He was inactive, uninvolved, and quiet as they rowed through their storm.

The disciples were fishermen, so this wasn't the first time they experienced a storm. But the Lord's quietness scared them.

It scares me, too. His silence in the middle of my storm causes me to feel like He doesn't care, and I'm perishing, too. Jesus didn't come saving the day and walking on the water this time for them. He was sleeping this time around.

I heard a saying once. I'm not sure where it comes from: "A teacher is the most quiet when the student is taking a test." This is true.

We can see it with the disciples. I can hear, "This is a test. This is only a test." Their teacher (Jesus) was asleep and quiet at the bottom of the boat, and they wavered in the midst of the storm. He was with them through the storm even though He was asleep, and His presence should have given them peace. But it didn't.

I asked the Lord a similar thing. "Lord, do You care about what I'm going through?" And it seemed like He was quiet, inactive in my life when I needed Him the most, in the midst of my endo storms. I wondered if He was sleeping.

God is with us while we go through our storms. He is present, not AWOL. And though He may seem silent, *His silence doesn't mean that He doesn't care.* He really does care. The Lord Himself watches over me and you.[25] He is there in the midst of our storms, active, involved and concerned. I don't quite understand it, but the Lord likes showing up in storms. (See Daniel 3; Matthew 14:24-25).

No matter how I feel today or tomorrow, the God of the Universe doesn't sleep or slumber. He's wide awake, and He stands beside me and you as a protective shade. He cares. He is strong enough to handle the weight of my cares. He wants my cares. And I will cast (throw) my cares upon Him, for He cares for me.[26]

I must throw my cares like a ball. My husband taught me how to throw a football. He showed me how to place my fingers on the white laces, cock my hand back, and step forward to throw the ball. I threw it forcefully toward him. And that's how I must do my cares. I must cast them. Throw them. And get rid of them.

Do you need to cast (throw) some cares, too? See yourself cocking your hand back behind your head and stepping forward. Now, forcefully throw all your cares upon the Lord like you would a ball or clothes into a washer or dryer. You're a good thrower, and *He is a great catcher.* He can handle the weight of your cares. Now, see Him catching your cares and perfecting that which concerns you.

Here's what I'm asking God...

God, you never slumber nor sleep. You, yourself watch over me as my protective shade. Let me not be shaken, afraid or moved by Your silence as I go through the storms of life. Make me aware of Your presence in the midst of the storm like You were with Your disciples, Daniel, Shadrach, Meshach, Abednego and so many others in their storms. I declare: I will get rid of my cares and throw them on the Lord.

Here's something to think on...

God is wide awake and His care has preserved your spirit.
(Job 10:12; Psalm 121:4-5).

Here's a tip to help you stand...

Have a casting off party. (Remember "cast" means to get rid of, place upon, throw upon forcefully.)

LETTER 22

Lord, Help My Unbelief

"When in doubt, get out of it and believe."[27]
~Chavos B.

Dear *Woman*,

I'm a doubting Thomasina, kin to the famous "Doubting Thomas." I want to believe and not doubt that one day I will be healed from my sickness. It's hard when the symptoms stare me in the face month after month. I know the Bible says, "...without faith it's impossible to please God." (Hebrews 11:6).

I like to think that I have faith, but I have some unbelief, too. I had faith that He would heal others from their illness, but not me. I had faith for my friends to get pregnant, but when it came time to believe for myself, I couldn't. I was certain, confident and sure He would come through for those I prayed for.

However, my requests fell short of confidence and surety. This is where I was a doubting Thomasina. Double-minded. How could I believe that God would heal others, but not me? I know this sounds strange, but maybe you've experienced the same thing. It's easy to believe for others, but very hard to believe for myself.

There was a man whose son was demon possessed. The father sought help and healing for his son from Jesus. (See Mark 9:17-28). I imagine he heard from others about how a carpenter by the name of Jesus healed them from their sickness, caused them to walk again, restored their sight and raised their children back to life. He probably heard testimony after testimony. And he probably received many recommendations, "You should take your boy to see Jesus. He healed me, and I heard He has healed others, too."

The man quickly ran to Jesus with expectation in his heart. He first met Jesus's disciples, and they couldn't heal the boy from a mute spirit. He hoped for change, and the boy remained the same. This man was probably discouraged and disappointed. Maybe this caused unbelief to settle in his heart—a little. Or maybe it started years ago.

Who knows what he tried before he got to Jesus and His disciples? It doesn't tell us, but somewhere unbelief came in. This man was probably at the end of his hope. Jesus was his last hope of ever having a healed son.

Now he stood before Jesus. This man had heard previous healing stories about Jesus and experienced the non-healing story of his son from the disciples of Jesus. He's face to face with his unbelief. "Could Jesus do the same for his child like He did for others?" Should he try one more time despite what didn't happen with His disciples?

He gave it one more try. He gave Jesus the 4-1-1 on how he brought his boy to His disciples and how they couldn't help him.

Jesus asked the man, "How long has this been happening to him?"

He answered, "Since he was a little boy. The spirit often throws him into the fire or into water, trying to kill him. Have mercy on us and help us, if you can." He was still uncertain if Jesus could help him.

"What do you mean, 'If I can?'" Jesus asked. "Anything is possible if a person believes.

"Immediately the father of the child cried out and said with tears, 'Lord, I believe; help my unbelief.'"[28]

To me, the man's response is double-minded. But if I take a closer look, it's not. He declared his belief and then asked for help for his unbelief. He was aware, open and honest to Jesus, and that's all it took. That one statement, and Jesus healed the man's son.

Lord, Help My Unbelief

I went for years unaware there was unbelief in my heart. So I didn't ask for help because I thought I believed. I believed, but somewhere after being prayed for over the same issue many times, changing my diet, going to different doctors, and with each failed home remedy and medication, negative doctors' report, returned fibroids and continued symptoms, unbelief settled in my heart.

Have you been to specialist after specialist? Healing line after healing line? And nothing's changed. Surgery after surgery? Shot after shot? And nothing's changed. Medication after medication? Prayer after prayer? And nothing's changed. Unbelief pitches a tent and camps out right next to the unchanged circumstances.

Do you need help with doubt and unbelief? If so, it's not a big deal. I sure do. I need heavenly aid with my unbelief. The first step of getting help is being aware and admitting we need help.

Wherever the unbelief came from, it really doesn't matter. All we need to say is, *"Lord, I believe, help my unbelief."* At first, I felt bad to admit that I had unbelief, but then I remembered the story of the man and his son.

God doesn't look down on us in disappointment because of our unbelief. He brings it to the light and allows us to face it, and confess that we have doubt and unbelief. He not only brings it to the light, but He helps us. The Lord is gracious and faithful to assist us in believing. And when we say that simple statement to him, He comes in and moves on our behalf and things change.

Here's what I'm asking God...

Lord, I believe, help my unbelief. It's easy for me to believe You for others, but when it comes to me it is a little difficult. You are the same God who moved to heal others. You don't have favorites whom You will heal, and others you will not heal. I want to believe You will do the same in my life. Let not doubt and unbelief be in my heart. I no longer want to be a Thomasina. Remove any double-mindedness from me, and cause me to be stable in my emotions and heart. I declare whatever things I ask when I pray, I believe that I will receive them, and I will have them. (Mark 11:24).

Here's something to think on...

Limitations, restrictions and hindrances can't stop a believing person.
(Mark 9:23; 11:23).

Here's a tip to help you stand...

Doubt your doubts, and use that same belief you have for others on yourself. Apply belief ointment to doubt and unbelief by speaking and declaring the Word of God. Let your prayer be, "Lord, I believe, help my unbelief." Believe for the impossible for the next fourteen days, thirty days or a year.

LETTER 23

I'm PMSing

"It wasn't me, the PMS made me do it."
~Chavos B.

Dear *Woman*,

I snapped at my husband for no reason.

My beloved husband stared at me from across the room. "Chavos, did I do something wrong?"

"No, you didn't do anything wrong. I'm PMSing." He didn't do anything wrong at *that* time. Everything seem to be magnified and annoying.

"Oh okay, I knew something was going on with you."

He was right. He wasn't being a male chauvinist like some men, who think women are PMSing 24/7. Something was really going on with me. I had an attitude, and my mood had changed in seconds.

Premenstrual Syndrome (PMS) causes my emotions to run loose like a wild animal. I'm moody. I crave chocolate-pudding-filled pies and chocolate donuts. My jeans are too tight, that's usually because I'm bloated, and I have premenstrual cramps. I have all kinds of aches: headaches, backaches, and my breasts are sore. Oh, did I mention that I'm tired.

Yep, these are all real signs of PMS. Can you relate to what I'm going through? It comes from out of nowhere. But not really! It comes like clockwork a couple days or weeks before "flo" comes, and it causes me to act like I'm losing my mind and becoming the "evil wife" from hell sometimes. I let PMS have control over my emotions, which causes me to do and to say anything. It's the puppet master of my emotions, and it takes them wherever it pleases.

PMS is real, but it wasn't an excuse for me to act the way I did. My poor beloved husband had nothing but grace for me all these years after his schooling on women and their periods.

I didn't like how my emotions and moodiness changed my personality as if I had a testy twin. I yielded to PMS's will and commands each month. It was my master, and I was its slave. I was tired of being under the influence of PMS's control. I couldn't help it; even when I wanted to be nice it came out mean.

I started to seek the Lord about the effects of PMS, and how I could bring it under the control of the Holy Spirit. He helped me combat PMS with fruit. I'm not talking about apples, oranges, pears and grapes, but the fruit of the Spirit: love, joy, peace, faithfulness, goodness, self-control, kindness, long-suffering and gentleness.[29] It hates fruit; it wants processed sugary sweet stuff. I like that stuff, but it wasn't helping.

When I feel like the premenstrual syndrome wants to have free reign in my mind and take my emotions on a wild bull ride, I *pray* for my emotions, my attitude and my mouth to be tamed. I *meditate* on the Word of God that talks about our emotions, thoughts, the mind of Christ, and having a gentle and quiet spirit. I *ask* God for help during my menstrual time. I ask for grace and for the law of kindness to be upon my lips. And I ask for the Holy Spirit to comfort me.

Out of this process came another meaning of PMS for me. It now meant Prayer, Meditation and Supplication. By doing these three things, I became more sweet and tender to deal with during and around my periods—for which my husband was grateful. My husband began to notice the difference in me. "You're not moody, and you're sweeter on your periods," he said. This was a long process that took several years because that premenstrual syndrome puppeteer didn't want to lose its grip on my emotions. But now I've become the puppeteer over my emotions, and they take orders from me.

I'm called to rule and conquer, and so are you. We know how to rule our own spirits, don't we?[30] I'm a queen, and you're a queen. We are daughters of the King. We look like our Daddy, slow to anger and slow to speak. We walk in grace, speaking kindness and showing mercy. So, I'm still PMSing, but in a different way: PRAYING-MEDITATING-SUPPLICATING.

Here's what I'm asking God...

God, I need Your divine assistance during my menstrual time. You have given me the power and grace to control my emotions. Let the fruit of the Holy Spirit be evident in my life to all those around me. Let not pre-menstrual syndrome rule my emotions and send me into fits of anger. Let the law of kindness be upon my lips, and if I can't say something kind, set a guard over my mouth. Holy Spirit, come as the divine helper. I declare PMS will not rule nor control my emotions, but I will walk in self-control and have a gentle and quiet spirit.

Here's something to think on...

A gentle and quiet spirit is precious to God. (1 Peter 3:4).

Here's a tip to help you stand...

Pray, Meditate and Supplicate: Cut the strings to the "PMS" puppeteer, and combat it with the fruit of the Spirit. (See Galatians 5:22-26). Watch your mood, emotions and words to see how you act. I dare you to say a kind word or two daily.

LETTER 24

Shame, Shame, Shame

"In You, O Lord, I put my trust; Let me never be put to shame."
~David (Psalm 71:1).

Dear *Woman*,

Have you heard of the hand clapping game? Shame, Shame, Shame. It goes:

> *"Shame, Shame, Shame*
> *I don't want to go to Mexico*
> *No more, more, more*
> *There's a big fat policeman*
> *At the door, door, door*
> *He grabbed me by the collar*
> *Made me pay a dollar*
> *I don't want to go to Mexico*
> *No more, more, more*
> *SHAME!"*

Maybe you played it as a child, or maybe you never heard of it. It was a very popular game among kids when I was growing up. I liked the hand-clapping part; it was fun. But as I think about the words now as an adult, the words were not so fun. What a horrible game called "Shame" to play and speak as a child.

Shame is not a game, nor is it a fun playful matter. I have experienced shame with dealing with the incurable disease of "endo-evil" (endometriosis).

Dear Woman

And I was unaware of this shame hidden in the closet of my heart until one day a conversation with my husband knocked down the door.

I was scheduled to speak at a meeting, but couldn't due to my regular endo episodes. I sent an email and a text to cancel, but didn't give the reason why. They responded, "Is everything okay?" I stared at the text for a while, trying to figure out how to answer that question.

My beloved husband said, "Just tell them what's going on with you."

I stared at him and back at the text, rereading, "Is everything okay?"

"Why should I tell them?" I said. I thought, they wouldn't understand if I told them anyway. So it's better to leave it unsaid.

"Why don't you share how you're feeling and open up to others? Is it because you don't trust anyone?" My beloved husband was trying hard to figure out what my deal was. You see these people were close friends, friends that I minister with often. He didn't understand why I didn't want to share with them.

"No, that's not it!" Now I was defensive and a little upset that he would say that to me. I trust people with certain things, but not with this issue. I hadn't opened up to anyone outside of my family regarding endo. Now, someone was asking me was I okay, and I didn't know how to respond.

"Are you ashamed of your illness?" my beloved said.

Bingo. That was it. His question was like an arrow. It hit the red painted target in the center of my heart. My tears gushed out like a broken fire hydrant.

He walked over to me and put his arms around me and held me tight. I sobbed in his arms soaking up his white-and-red-striped shirt with my tears.

The sheets of shame were snatched off and uncovered that day, and could no longer play hide-and-seek in my heart and mind anymore. God had shone His light on the real issue.

Shame is secretive. It whispers, "Shhh…don't tell anyone! If they knew about your condition, they would judge you and think you are weird. Look, see, you're not normal. Something is wrong with you." Shame likes the dark and hates the light. Shame likes to be alone and isolated. It causes us to hide and cover ourselves because of the fear of being misunderstood and the lack of understanding and knowledge of the illness we face. Shame made me think that people thought I was crazy or lying.

Shame made me think I was the only one going through it, and I was abnormal. Shame made me feel embarrassed about going through endo episodes and caused me to question, "Why couldn't I be normal like other women or girls? Why do I miss important events because of this issue?

Are you familiar with shame? Have you heard, "Shame, Shame, Shame on you?" If so, no more shame! I heard a lady preaching one day by the name of Trisha Frost say, "*Shame off you.*" That stayed with me. I declare that over us, "Shame off us in the name of Jesus."

Let shame's address no longer be in our hearts, minds and souls. Let shame's garment be cast off of us. Let shame's disgrace be replaced by double honor. Double *honor* is coming to you and to me, and it will replace and overshadow all the shameful years.

Here's what I'm asking God...

God, in you I put my trust. Let me never be put to shame. Let the light of your countenance shine on my heart revealing any pockets of shame or embarrassment. Break the spirit of shame off of me and close my ears to its lies. Cause me to forget the shame of dealing with my condition. Surround me with Your love and comfort, and remove all reproach from me, and give me double honor for years of shame. I declare I will not fear, for what can man do to me. I will not be ashamed, neither disgraced, for I will not be put to shame. (Isaiah 54:4).

Here's something to think on...

Your shame will be replaced with double honor. (Isaiah 61:7).

Here's a tip to help you stand...

Shine the flashlight on shame, and drag it out of the closet and expose it (share it with a close friend, trusted family member, pastor, or mentor).

LETTER 25

God Must Be Mad At Me

*"The Lord is gracious and full of compassion,
slow to anger and great in mercy."*
~David (Psalm 145:8).

Dear *Woman*,

God is mad at me. I've sinned big time. I cut off that person on the highway. I mouthed off at my parents as a teenager or an adult. I haven't been to church in a month. Oh, I know, I didn't help that person on the side of the road. Maybe I still have unforgiveness against that person who hurt me. Man, I sped up on the highway so no one would get in front of me. I got a nasty attitude with my husband. I talked about so-and-so behind her back. I let that compliment go to my head. I disobeyed my parents. I was promiscuous and wild back in the day. Oh, no, I forgot to read my Bible and pray today. For sure, God must be mad at me now. "Oooh, you're gonna get it now, girl."

I sat and rehearsed all the known sins I could remember, justifying why God had the right to be mad at me. You thought you were the only one who thought or felt like this? Nope. You're not alone. I think it comes with the territory. Sickness has a way of making us think we did something wrong. I repented, begged and apologized for everything I knew I had done. What more could I've done to make the wrath of God stop in my life?

My situations drew a false picture of an angry God on the throne with long white hair sticking straight out, with a lightning bolt in His right hand and steam coming from His ears and head. The look on His face was one of displeasure and disgust. Who would want to approach a God like that? That was the false image I had, so different from how He really is—a *loving* Father.

God is not mad at you or me. He's "madly" (over-the-top passionately) involved in my life and yours, too. His face isn't frowned up toward you or me with mean, thick, heavy eyebrows looking down on us over His glasses with His big arms crossed and tapping His foot on heaven's floor. Even though our situations cause us to feel like He's this way toward us. He is so far from being mad at you or me. He is so far from being like an earthly father or friend. He is so far from being a Mr. Scrooge or the Grinch.

He's a *glad* God. Can you picture the God of the Universe singing over you? What? God sings? Yep. God, our Father is the Singing God. He surrounds us with songs of deliverance and freedom. And rejoices over us with singing.[31]

Can you picture His bright white teeth showing with His cheeks raised? Can you picture His eyes full of light and gladness? Can you picture Him kneeling with one leg down and the other bent, holding out His arms to us as a loving Father wanting us to run into His arms? This is His posture toward you and me. That's the kind of God I can approach. So, let's run into the loving arms of our *joyous* Father.

God Must Be Mad at Me

Here's what I'm asking God...

God, what I'm going through causes me to think You are mad at me for something I did or didn't do. Help me to realize and see the truth. Heal my image of You, and cause me to see You as the singing, laughing, joyous God and a *glad* Father. Let me hear You singing over me. I renounce the false image of You as the angry God toward me, and I accept Your love for me. You are slow to anger, full of compassion, showing lovingkindness to all your children.

Here's something to think on...

God loves you with an everlasting love and draws you with lovingkindness. (Jeremiah 31:3).

Here's a tip to help you stand...

Ask God to give you a vision of Him—joyous, and open your ears to hear His song over you. Close your eyes and imagine God happy, laughing and delighted in you. Imagine God smiling and joyous over you with His arms held out to you.

LETTER 26

Please, No More Suffering

> "Here on earth you will have many trials and sorrows. But take heart, because I have overcome the world."
> ~Jesus (John 16:33 NLT).

Dear *Woman*,

I wish I was a superhero. I would be Endometra Girl, and my power would stop suffering, battle pain, and calm cramps. I wish I had a magic wand to make all your suffering stop and to send you to a distant land called "suffer-less land," where life is pleasant, no troubles, no worries and no pain. But I can't. My heart goes out to you.

You know, I wanted to escape my endo suffering and go to a distant land. But there was no Endometra Girl in sight to wave her wand over me to make the suffering stop. I only had a thought, "Why don't you just go get a hysterectomy? Be done with it and forget about trying to have kids." I considered this for several days. I didn't tell anyone—not even my husband—my thoughts about getting a non-medically-required-voluntary-hysterectomy. I wasn't ready for the conversation yet.

But in the back of my mind, I thought what about the promises from God about kids. Did God lie (I know He can't lie), or was I impatient? I didn't want to suffer anymore. Who wants to suffer? No one volunteers to wake each day and say, "Hey, I would like to suffer today. Bring it on."

I wanted to be done with suffering at the cost of maybe not being able to have kids. I wanted to be done with the misery of my "monthly." I wanted to be done with the pain, pads and periods. Each month I wanted this vicious cycle to end that drove me crazy at times, made me cry and depressed. Like a period at the end of a sentence, I was done. I didn't want to take it anymore. I thought having a hysterectomy would end it all.

There were several issues standing in the way of my idea: my family, the desire to have children and the fact that it wasn't medically required. This wrestle with a voluntary hysterectomy was a big issue for me because my mother had a doctor-required hysterectomy at age 33. She hadn't wanted a hysterectomy; she had to get one because of what it was doing to her insides. Whereas it wasn't a medical reason for me at age 33 (my heart goes out to those who had to have a medically required hysterectomy). It was my way of trying to cure or end endo once and for all. (I've recently heard that a hysterectomy isn't the cure).

Eventually, I had to fess up to my family and tell them. My mother reminded me about the promises of God. She said, "I know what the Lord showed me, and He promised you children. You know this is not the will of God for you if there is no medical reason, and the doctors aren't requiring it. There is no reason to have one." My husband reminded me about the promises of God, too. I knew what they said was right, and I knew it also meant embracing a season of suffering.

God never promised that there wouldn't be suffering. I wish that were the case. But Jesus told us, "In this world you will have trouble." (John 16:33 NIV). He was right. Trouble there is, and suffering there is. But God reveals Himself and things about us in the midst of suffering.

I don't like to suffer. It's not the most desirable situation, but it's like a teacher. Hebrews 5:8 says, "He (Jesus) learned obedience by the things which He suffered." God, couldn't He have learned by another way? God, can I learn by another way? Please, no more suffering. But if I look back over these past ten years, suffering has taught me. It's taught me mercy, compassion, how to relate, sensitivity, faith, endurance and more. I wouldn't have gained this without suffering. Did I write that out loud? Yep, I did, and it's the truth, though it doesn't feel good.

Please, No More Suffering

Are you suffering right now? What are you learning? Where is your distant land that you escape to? I know the tendency is to want to escape. I tried to run from it, but I ended up learning from it. We have the grace and the stamina to endure this. God made you to endure this. How do I know? Because you're around to read this. You still find a way to smile. Give a hug. Sing a song. Enjoy a good book or movie. Take yourself shopping. Get dressed and live.

God is working something in us. He's making us heavyweights in the spirit and pure vessels to be able to hold the glory. We can comfort others during their times of suffering because we know what it's like. May you experience the abundant grace of God to endure this suffering. In the midst of your suffering know there are others who are suffering along through their journey, too.

Here's what I'm asking God...

God of all comfort, it doesn't feel pleasant or good to suffer. I'd love for it to end, but You told us there will be trouble in this life. You said, "Let not your hearts be troubled." Cause my heart to be at peace, and give me perseverance like Job. Look upon those who are suffering and in worse conditions than me. Give me grace to walk through this and learn from it. I declare God hears my cry and sees my afflictions.

Here's something to think on...

Today's or tomorrow's sufferings fall short compared to the future glory He will reveal in us. (Romans 8:18).

Here's a tip to help you stand...

Pray. (See James 5:13). Do you know someone who is worse off than you? If so, call or visit them and pray for them. Give a hug, a smile, a card or flowers. If not, talk with God about your suffering.

LETTER 27

New Mercies

"The faithful love of the Lord never ends! His mercies never cease. Great is His faithfulness; His mercies begin afresh (new) each morning."
~Moses (Lamentations 3:22-23 NLT).

Dear *Woman*,

Do you like new things? I like new stuff. Who doesn't like getting new stuff? New clothes, new shoes, new furniture, a new house, or new career. New things like clothes have a way of making a person feel better and make them walk differently. New things are exciting and intriguing, and we want to spend time using them and trying out the new things.

My husband likes gadgets, and when he gets a new phone I lose him for a couple of hours. He spends time playing with it and trying out all the new features. When my husband gets anything new whether it's a new gadget or new shoes he will wear it out, especially his shoes until he can see the bottom of his socks through the soles.

After a while the once-new outfit, phone, shoes, house, job or furniture is now old, outdated, and familiar. The newness is gone...we wear out the newness from over usage. It never can become new again.

Have you ever forged a new friendship? In the beginning you were excited, inquisitive and careful not to offend. You wanted to make a good impression and spend a lot of time getting to know the person. After a while, the newness of the relationship wears off, and you began to see flaws, inconsistencies, pet peeves, dislikes, the bad and ugly imperfections. You start to feel the relationship is worn out.

I learned that mercy is similar; it starts out new, but then it's old by the end of the day. When our heads hit the pillow, mercy is old, outdated, drained and familiar. It's different from material things in that it becomes brand new the next day.

"Morning by morning new mercies I see; all I have needed His hand has provided. Great is His faithfulness unto me."* These lyrics are from a popular song about the mercies of God and one of my favorites. I wish I could say I hear this song or even realize His new mercies each day. But I don't.

Morning by morning, I usually hear the sound of my husband's annoying alarm clock going off. Beep, beep, beep, beep.

"Good morning, Beauty," says my beloved husband. He leans over to hit the snooze button on his cell phone. Great, I will hear that stupid alarm clock again in fifteen minutes, snatching me out of dreamland.

Morning by morning, it takes me a while to stir. I would prefer to wake up on my own without the unpleasant sounds coming from the alarm clock. I finally emerge from under my comforter, flinging it off me. I sit up and slip my feet into my blue-and-pink fluffy house shoes and head off to the bathroom.

Morning by morning, I shower, wash my face, brush my teeth and get dressed. And I'm off to start my day. But wait, I forgot something. I didn't realize I woke up today with something "new" waiting for me. Something new called "*mercy.*"

Mercy today isn't like yesterday's mercies because it is for whatever we'll face today. God gives us new mercies tailor-made and sufficient for the day. He knew we'd wear out mercy like someone wears a hole in their shoes or a like a battery on a cell phone because we need a lot of mercy. So He worked in our Daily Destiny Plan to give us new Mercy Minutes each morning. What a generous God! He could let mercy expire, and then where would I be? But He supplies it unlimited and for eternity.

---

*Taken from "Great Is Thy Faithfulness" by Thomas O. Chisholm © 1923. Ren. 1951 Hope Publishing Company, Carol Stream, IL 60188. Used by permission. www.hopepublishing.com. All rights reserved.

New Mercies

We might not wake each morning to new things like clothes, shoes or gadgets, which would be nice. But we do wake each morning with brand new mercies, which are ready to be unwrapped, tried out, enjoyed, and used as much as we please in our life. We can run boldly, with confidence to the throne of grace to obtain mercy and find help in the time of need.[32] For great is His mercy toward you and me.

Here's what I'm asking God...

God, great is Your faithfulness. Thank you for Your fresh new mercies toward me every morning. Make me aware and sensitive to new mercies I will walk in today. You show compassion according to the multitude of Your mercies. For Your mercy follows me all the days of my life. I declare I walk in new mercies each morning, and mercy surrounds me because I trust in the Lord. (Psalm 32:10).

Here's something to think on...

If mercy was on Twitter it would follow you. (Psalm 23:6).

Here's a tip to help you stand...

Unwrap and tryout mercy each morning. Make a reminder (like a note on the wall, a screensaver on your phone or computer or send yourself a text message).

IV. Seen By Jesus

LETTER 28

Daughter of Abraham

> "For indeed He does not give aid to angels, but He does give aid to the seed of Abraham."
> ~(Hebrews 2:16).

Dear *Woman*,

Who's your daddy? Abraham is your daddy, the father of faith, who stood and trusted God in the face of negative circumstances. You're a daughter of Abraham, and not only are you a daughter of Abraham, but *you are a daughter of God*. And because you're Abraham's daughter you have the capacity to stand like Abraham and trust God in the face of your symptoms, doctor reports, pain, discomforts, disappointments, hurts, or whatever you're facing right now.

Daughters of Abraham—this is our *true* identity and how God sees you and me. However, along our journeys we must deal with a chronic illness and challenging situations and storms that come like a thief, snatching our purposes and stealing our identities. This thief tries to define us and speak over us a false identity.

Our *"dear woman"* friend (in Luke 13) had her identity stolen by her illness. People probably didn't see her as a daughter of Abraham. They probably thought, "Who her? A daughter of Abraham? Please. I don't think so! Abraham wasn't bent over. Abraham wasn't sickly. Abraham wasn't crippled. She's useless and helpless and needs much assistance."

But it didn't matter what others thought about her. Jesus spoke to who she really was and not to what her situation said she was. He declared her true identity.

Endo is a thief, and it tried to steal my identity from me several times, which caused me to think I was less than who God said I was. It made me think I was less than a woman. It made me think I was an incapable person. It made me think I was alone, abandoned and an orphan.

"God has left you to suffer with this disease all by yourself. You're not strong, you're weak"—these are the lies I heard. Endo was speaking falsehood to me, but it was easy to believe. Sometimes fatigue, weariness from the battle, and physical pain can cause a weak point in our shields. It was hard to discern between the real and the counterfeit or between the truth and the lie.

Endo slowly took my identity. I was confused and disillusioned, "Who am I? Am I the girl with "Stage Four Endo"? Am I the girl, who is homebound and friends with her bed for three days straight of each month? Who am I?"

The Lord speaks over you and me, "You are my daughter. You are a child of promise. You are from the seed of Abraham."

What does it mean to be a daughter of Abraham? Abraham was a man of faith. He trusted God in the midst of a barren situation. God told him, "Look now toward heaven, and count the stars if you are able to number them." (Genesis 15:5). Abraham gazed toward a heaven lit with stars. And God said, "So shall your descendants be."

When he didn't have a son, Abraham believed and stayed in faith for a seed one day. He's part of the "Hall of Faith." We are his seed, and nothing can take that away from us. We can't help but hope when hope tries to escape us. We face down our sickness, fears, afflictions, and unfulfilled promises with eyes of faith. We dare to stand and just believe God because it's in our blood, and you and I will join Abraham and others in the "Hall of Faith."

We believe and know this is our *true* identity in whatever situation we find ourselves. And whatever Abraham, the great "hall-of-faither" experienced, you and I will experience because we are his daughters, and we have his "faith DNA."

Like Abraham, you and I are standing and trusting in our God in the face of our circumstances, illnesses, hardships and trials. We speak as women —women who know their identities with boldness, confidence, and faith in one voice declaring, "I'm a daughter of Abraham. I'm a daughter of God."

Here's what I'm asking God...

God, I am in Christ, and I am a seed of Abraham. I believe all things are possible by You, my God. Let my faith in You and what You have spoken and promised be accounted to me for righteousness like Abraham. I declare by faith, I will trust and believe even when I can't see my way or positive results. For I walk by faith and not by sight.

Here's something to think on...

The seed of Abraham is blessed because of Abraham. (Galatians 3:29).

Here's a tip to help you stand...

Who's your daddy? Buy or make a name tag...<u>Hello my name is</u> or <u>I am a "Daughter of Abraham."</u> Type or write out faith declarations. Complete this statement - By faith...(according to Hebrews 11). What will you do by faith?

My declaration: By faith I will push past my fears, doubts and resistance and write my story for God's glory. Your turn...By faith I will...

LETTER 29

Dear Woman

"Many daughters have done well, but you excel them all."
~King Lemuel's Mother (Proverbs 31:29).

Dear *Woman*,

Aren't you thankful for being a woman? I am. No matter the ups and downs or aches and achievements. No matter the pain and pleasure, or purpose and pressure. No matter the hills and valleys or heels and clutches. I'm glad to be a woman. Not just any woman—a dear woman, who is special to the heart of God. God loves women.

We have a place in the world to shine our light and decorate the world with love, laughter, joy, nurture, wisdom, support, and creativity. We know how to decorate, don't we? It's just something that is in us. We see an empty wall or house, and it is our big canvas to make it a beautiful home. We are artists, and we create something beautiful for our family and friends to enjoy.

You and I are something special. God took some time with you and me. He took mother Eve from father Adam's rib, not from the dirt. And we are the best of the best. He formed you in your mother's womb and put purpose, calling, gifting, and talents inside of you. Your inward parts were intricately made by the Creator. You and I are fearfully and wonderfully made masterpieces, even though we may not feel wonderful all the time.

You are wise. You have the grace and wisdom to carry out a plan and vision. You have foresight about how to prepare for the future and insight and discernment to see things for what they truly are. You have the skill to understand the seasons and how to properly plan for them. Your household doesn't suffer lack. You ponder the path of your feet and know the way of wisdom.

God has graced us with inner beauty with a gentle and quiet spirit that is precious to Him and spills out on the outside. You are a *bad* (slang for good) dresser. You've clothed yourself in strength and honor.[33] And the robe of humility is your garment of choice. You run from evil and at the first sound of slander or gossip, you're out the door or ready to address and redirect the conversation.

You are kind, and you have a way to craft and form words to encourage, motivate and kindly correct, speaking the truth coated in love. You speak words of kindness to those around you, and on your lips is the law of kindness.[34] You give a helping hand to those in need. You give wise and sound advice. You're a counselor one day and a doctor another, taking care of sick little people, yourself, or a loved one. You nurture, train and coach all kinds of people (little people and big people). You have the ability to build up and encourage others, making them feel special.

We are *dear* to God. We are His beloved. He can share the secrets of His heart with you and me and trust us to keep them safe. We are His friends.[35] So, let's lean in closer to hear what He has to say and share with us because we are valuable, and extremely important in partnering with Him and His plans.

Here's what I'm asking God...

Father, I praise you for you formed my inward parts (uterus, heart, lungs, intestine, soul, spirit, etc), "you covered me in my mother's womb, and I am fearfully and wonderfully made." Let me not be so concerned and obsessed over my physical appearance but fight to develop and show "the incorruptible beauty of a gentle and quiet spirit, which is precious in God's eyes. "For charm is deceitful and beauty is passing, but a woman who fears the Lord, she shall be praised." Lord, give me favor with You and man. Let me obtain favor in Your sight and in the sight of all who see me, like Esther. I declare, I will rejoice because I am God's highly favored one; the Lord is with me, and I am blessed among women. (Psalm 139:14; 1 Peter 3:4; Proverbs 31:29; Luke 1:42).

Here's something to think on...

God has a tattoo of you on His hand. (Isaiah 49:16 TLB).

Here's a tip to help you stand...

Set your timer for 60 seconds, and jot down everything that comes to mind about being fearfully and wonderfully made. Finish the sentence...I am woman, hear me...

LETTER 30

Jesus Sees You

"For the eyes of the Lord run to and fro throughout the whole earth, to show Himself strong on behalf of those whose heart is loyal to Him."
~Hanani (2 Chronicles 16:9).

Dear *Woman*,

Have you ever felt or caught someone staring at you? Did you know Jesus is staring straight at you? Girl, He's got His eyes on you. He sees you now in the state that you're in. He sees you on your good days when you're up, out and about running errands, laughing, and hanging out with family and friends. He sees you praying, singing or sewing and whatever activities you're involved in. Do you believe that? Jesus sees you, even if you don't think He does.

I didn't think He saw me. I questioned, "God do you see me? No, you don't see me." I assumed the God, Who made eyes, had closed His eyes to me, because if He saw me He'd come to my rescue. Or maybe His eyes were focused or busy on better and more important things than little ol' me and my situation. There are other people (His children) who request and need His attention, too.

It was naive of me to think He wasn't able to see me, see you, and see the woman in Asia all at the same time. God reminded me, "I'm not like man, Chavos. Man's vision is limited and restricted. I see all and know all, past, present and future, infinitely." He's looking at you and me, even when we're not asking for Him to look at us and when we are unaware of His watchful gaze.

Dear Woman

Our "*dear woman*" friend (in Luke 13) probably didn't recognize that Jesus was looking at her, or maybe she did. Maybe she heard stories of how He healed the woman with the twelve-year-long issue of blood or raised a governor's daughter back to life or how He made a man's withered hand straight. And now Jesus stands and teaches in the temple the same day she was there.

Can you picture it? Jesus was walking back and forth teaching with power and authority? And then His eyes fell upon the *dear woman*. His gaze wasn't one of lust, but one of compassion, love and mercy.

In a bent-over posture, she probably was barely able to look at anyone's eyes. Her eyes faced the floor as she walked. But it was different this day. Jesus saw her, and she was no longer ignored or overlooked. She was seen. His focus and attention was on her to move on her behalf, and to deliver her from her present situation.

The "*dear woman*" was in the synagogue when Jesus saw her. Where are you today? Are you at home? Are you at the hospital? At the store? In the car? At the park? In church? At the airport? At the library? Wherever you are, Jesus sees you just like He looked at our dear friend. Jesus's eyes like fire were full of passion and compassion staring at this woman. And His eyes are the same today, staring at you.

He is the seeing God, who saw her long history of being bound, crippled, ill, and everything that caused her to be in that state. He saw her, and He sees you. There is nothing hidden from His sight, and all things are laid bare before God.[36] When Jesus's eyes fell upon her all things were opened and revealed, and nothing was hidden from Him. His eyes have fallen upon you and me, too.

Jesus sees you and me, in our lying, sitting or bent-over position. He sees the years you've been dealing with endometriosis or another illness. And even though endo is a hidden silent disease and may not be visible to the eyes of man, it doesn't get past the gaze of Jesus. He sees the loss, the pain, the hurt, the disappointment, the fibroids, the cancer cells, and the shame. He sees it all with eyes like flames of fire melting away the icy storms and cold, hard places. He looks at you and me with love, passion and compassion.

He is not ignorant of your state. His eyes aren't closed. The delay or lack of answer to your situation doesn't mean He doesn't see you. I wonder, how many times Jesus visited the synagogue? Was this lady always there? Imagine with me, what if she went to the synagogue and saw Jesus year after year from the time He was twelve. It was not yet time for His healing ministry to begin at age twelve, but eighteen years later here He was preaching again in the temple. His eyes connected with hers, and the fullness of time came for her.

The fullness of time will come for you and for me. We can rest today knowing that Jesus sees us, and we aren't hidden from His sight. David said it like this, "Where can I flee from your presence?"[37] We can never go too far outside the vision range of the God, who created sight. *His gaze* is continually locked on us.

Here's what I'm asking God...

God, you sit enthroned on high, but You stoop down to look low upon us. And nothing is hidden from Your gaze. My ways, thoughts and life are not hidden from You. You see everything that concerns my life. "You are the God who sees me."[38] Look upon me and answer my prayers and my cry, O Lord. I declare the eyes of the Lord search to and fro and they find me with a loyal heart.

Here's something to think on...

Heaven's gaze is continually upon you. (Psalm 34:15).

Here's a tip to help you stand...

Word challenge: How many scriptures can you find about the eyes of the Lord? Close your eyes and imagine His eyes on you or go outside and look up in the sky, imagine Him looking back upon you.

LETTER 31

Jesus Calls You

"...I have called you by your name; you are mine."
~God (Isaiah 43:1).

Dear *Woman*,

"Take a number, have a seat, and your number will be called shortly." Have you ever heard this? I grab a blue ticket from the red ticket dispenser attached to the wall and look down at the number, "Man, I'm number 52." I look over at the black digital number counter that shows the magical red number and it reads "45." It's going to be a while.

I intently watch the black digital counter on the wall like it's a blockbuster movie, and I hope for the big climax of when my number is called. After several minutes and clicks, they finally reach my number. They call out, "Number 52, Number 52." I stand up, shout and raise my hand like I'm back in kindergarten class to get their attention before they quickly switch to the next number. My number is called, and it's a good feeling to finally get help, to be called and acknowledged.

Our "*dear woman*" friend (in Luke 13) must have felt really good on the day she was called. I picture her bent over sitting on a hard cement or wooden bench, with her arms on her knees listening intently to every word Rabbi Jesus was teaching. "Oh, how I wish He would call me out of the crowd and speak a word to me and pray for me to be healed." Jesus breaks into her thoughts, and right then He calls her over to him.

"Who, me?" She was shocked and surprised that He called and knew her name.

Jesus smiles and waits for her to come, holding out His hand to her. Now all eyes turn to look at her. "Why did Jesus only call her? What makes her so special? Doesn't he know she has a spirit of infirmity and can't even walk straight?"

He knew, and it didn't change His mind at all.

His invitation gave her the motivation to move. She mustered some strength to get up and walked doubled over toward him with her eyes downward.

Her number was called that day. How special it must have felt. Of all the people in the synagogue that day, who were sick and waiting and wanting their names to be called, she was the one He called.

You are called. God has your number, and He knows your name. He's calling you and me. He calls you out of the crowd of all the other women. Who you? Yep, you and me. And others might not understand why He's called and chosen you or me. "Why her?" They might ask. "Does He know she is…?"

"Doesn't He know her father left her when she was a child? Doesn't He know she can't even speak straight? Doesn't He know she has an illness? What makes her so special or different? Does He know she used to…?"

Yep.

He knows, and it doesn't change his invitation to us at all.

Can you hear the voice of Rabbi Jesus calling you to Himself? He calls you and me by our names. And He has a creative way He calls you, which is different from the way He calls me. There were those who went to Jesus on their own accord for healing, and then there were those He called to Himself. Jesus is calling us to Himself.

His call leads to action; change happens in the lives of the person He calls. His voice is powerful and thunderous; things shake, shift and quake at the sound of His voice. He called "blind Bartimaeus" to Himself, and Bartimaeus left with eyes wide open. He called Samuel, and he received a word and became a mighty mouthpiece for God. Jesus called the disciples to

Himself, and they went from being fishers of fish to fishers of men, who greatly impacted the world.

He calls you and me. You might be bent over double, too weak to stand, tired, fatigued, lonely, afraid, upset, uncertain, and unable to lift your gaze to heaven. It doesn't matter; He calls you to Himself. Jesus calls you and me to come to Him in our weakened position. Oh, what will happen in our lives after we respond to His call?

Here's what I'm asking God...

God, open my ears to Your voice, for You call me by my name, and I am Yours. I was created for Your glory and formed by Your hands. I will run to You. Help me to respond rightly when You call me. Thank you for calling me to Yourself. I declare I am known by God, and I have favor with Him and man.

Here's something to think on...
God called you before you were born. (Isaiah 49:1).

Here's a tip to help you stand...

Your name is important. Find out the meaning of your name (first, middle and last) and write a poem or inspirational piece or create a bookmark using the meaning of your name.

For fun: Make up a new name by merging your first name with your middle or last name or all three. (My example, Vos'An)

LETTER 32

The Lord of The Sabbath

> "Of how much more value then is a man than a sheep? Therefore it is lawful to do good on the Sabbath."
> ~Jesus (Matthew 12:12).

Dear *Woman*,

What if hospitals had a rule that no sick people could be helped or admitted on a certain day? That would be absolutely crazy. This would be a very strange rule for a hospital to have because its purpose and reason for existence is to help people. What would be the point?

What if the church had the same rule or law, too? What if in the middle of your chronic illness episodes you ran to your pastor for prayer? You know, doing what the Bible says, "If there be anyone sick among you, let them call on the elders for prayer, and they will pray the prayer of faith." (James 5:14).

What if you went to one of the elders or pastors of the church in horrible pain? And when you approached the front door of the church, there was a big red-and-yellow plastic sign that read: "We no longer pray for the healing of sick people on Sundays. Sorry for any inconvenience; please come back another day." You frown and ignore the sign, clearly thinking it must be a joke, even though it wasn't April 1st. You head to the Pastor's office and knock.

"Come in," the Pastor says through the old wooden door.

"Hello, Pastor." You shake his hand and topple down in his red-leather office chair.

"Hello, how can I help you?" His voice sounds kind and compassionate as if he were a waiter at a restaurant. You think for sure that sign was a joke because he seems too nice to put that sign up there.

"I'm experiencing debilitating pain, and I really need prayer." You expect him to do like the Bible says, right, and lay hands on you and pray the prayer of faith.

He says, "I'm sorry. I don't pray for people on this day. This is my day of rest and no work. Please come back another day for prayer." He stares at you in hope that you will understand.

You sit there staring back at him. "I thought it was always the right time to pray for someone—especially those who are sick or in need of prayer."

He stands up and walks over to the door and opens it. "I'm sorry...this is our new rule. I hope you can understand and accept our new process." He wants you to make a quick exit out of his office. "But please come back another day, if you can."

How would you feel? Would you go back to that church? I wouldn't go back. My search for a new place of worship would begin that day. I know this made-up scenario sounds extreme. I haven't run into any churches like this, and I hope you and I never do.

Our "*dear woman*" friend wasn't as fortunate as us. She attended a synagogue, much like a church, which had this type of rule in place when she was cured from her illness. She probably understood that when the Sabbath came around, don't dare think about going to ask the chief priest and elders for prayer. There was no big red-and-yellow sign that said "no healing." It was just the rule, and it was understood by everyone.

The elders, scribes, and Pharisees of the synagogues weren't concerned about praying for the people. Praying for the people should've been their major focus. Instead they were too concerned with shutting up the kingdom of heaven against men. They didn't go in or allow others to enter either. (See Matthew 23:13). They were too concerned with the traditions of men, rituals, and rules. They were too concerned with making sure the money changers were selling and happy.

They misinterpreted and twisted the law. The rule was no work of any kind on the Sabbath.³⁹ They assumed it meant no healing, too.

So, when Jesus constantly healed people on the Sabbath day the religious leaders were undone and outraged by His non-compliance with the Jewish Laws.

They confronted Jesus after he healed a man's hand, "...saying, 'Is it lawful to heal on the Sabbath?'—that they might accuse Him.

"Then He said to them, 'What man is there among you who has one sheep, and if it falls into a pit on the Sabbath, will not lay hold of it and lift it out? Of how much more value then is a man than a sheep? Therefore it is lawful to do good on the Sabbath.'" (Matthew 12: 9-14).

Jesus didn't come in the traditional way through the doctrine of men and systems set up by them. He kept healing on the so-called "no healing day." When he healed our *"dear woman"* friend, the religious leaders confronted him again because he healed on the Sabbath.

The leader told the crowd, "There are six days on which men ought to work; therefore come and be healed on them, and not on the Sabbath day."

"The Lord then answered him and said, 'Hypocrite! Does not each one of you on the Sabbath loose his ox or donkey from the stall, and lead it away to water it? So ought not this woman, being a daughter of Abraham, whom Satan has bound—think of it—for eighteen years, be loosed from this bond on the Sabbath?' And when He said these things, all His adversaries were put to shame; and all the multitude rejoiced for all the glorious things that were done by Him." (Luke 13:14-17).

The Lord of the Sabbath confronts, overthrows and breaks religious systems and man-made rules and scientific standards. He breaks natural laws, policies, limitations and restrictions to set His people free. He broke the "no healing day" law and healed our *"dear woman"* friend. There are *no off-limit* days for Him. She probably didn't expect it because she was restricted by the rules. That Sabbath day came as a day of restoration for her.

Your Sabbath day is coming, too. No matter what rules, restrictions, or limitations are put on us by man, science, others or ourselves that say, "You can't do this or that. You will always be this way. You should stop believing for a miracle. You can't be healed in your home." He confronts, overthrows and breaks those things, and comes to us anyway as the Lord of the Sabbath just like he did for the "*dear woman.*"

Here's what I'm asking God...

God, You are gracious and kind to me. You're not bound or restricted by man's traditions, rules or laws. But You break, confront and overthrow hindrances, limitations, systems and anything that will say, "no healing for me" or "no restoration for me" or "no peace for me." You are the Lord of the Sabbath; come and heal me today. I declare the Lord will do exceedingly abundantly above what I can ask or think according to the power that works in me. (Ephesians 3:20).

Here's something to think on...

Heaven is open for healing business 24/7, 365 days for all eternity.
(Luke 4:40).

Here's a tip to help you stand...

Mark your calendar, and save the date. Pencil in "The Lord of the Sabbath Day is coming to a home near me" in the subject line. Put it on your calendar on your phone or on paper as an event and expect Him to come.

LETTER 33

The Stripes of Jesus

"...He was afflicted, yet He opened not His mouth; He was led as a lamb to the slaughter, and as a sheep before its shearers is silent..."

~Isaiah (Isaiah 53:7).

Dear *Woman*,

Jesus, the man that never sinned, took a brutal beating at the hands of the Roman soldiers. He was innocent, perfect and spotless. They interrogated Him, spit in His face and mocked Him. The Bible doesn't give us detail by detail of Jesus's Roman beating. But when I close my eyes I picture this:

The Roman soldiers stripped Jesus's clothes from Him. They pushed a crown of thorns down on His head. The thorns pierced his skull, causing blood to drip down on his face and eyelids. Their weapon of choice was not an automatic weapon or knife, it was (likely) a 30-inch whip, made of sheep bones, nails, rocks and metal. It was called the "cat o' nine tails" or "the cat" for short.[40]

They laughed and boasted, "This is going to be some beating. We will get him good," as they sat twisting and knotting the leather whip mixed with sheep bones, nails, rocks and metal.

Someone asked, "Who is this guy?"

"They call him Jesus of Nazareth. The Jewish leaders brought him to see Pilate because he claims to be the Son of God." A soldier sneered.

"Really. Well, let's see if the Son of God can handle this." One of the Roman soldiers lifted up the homemade whip and cocked it back, swung it around and then forward—hitting, slashing, ripping the flesh of Jesus.

The soldier yelled out, "One." One of the nails connected with Jesus's flesh and tore all the way down his back. The Roman Soldier lifted the whip again with the same motion and swung. The whip connected with Jesus's flesh and ripped into it in another spot on his back. This time it caused a deep gash in his back.

"Two," he counted with each hit, "three, four, five, six, seven, eight, nine, ten," stopping to wipe blood from his own arm.

He continued, "fifteen, sixteen, seventeen..." He paused to fix a piece of leather on the whip. He continued, swinging the whip. "Twenty, twenty-one, twenty-two, twenty-three, twenty-four, twenty-five." I imagine his arms got heavy and tired like he'd been bench pressing. By now, the body of Jesus was horribly disfigured.

The soldier wiped more of the precious blood of the Lamb off his face and continued to count, "Thirty, thirty-one, thirty-two, thirty-three, thirty-four." The Roman Soldier could feel victory and the momentum and see the finish line. He was about to meet the Roman quota for beatings. He turned to look at his partners on the side, and they smiled and cheered him on and gave him the Roman sign of approval.

One of his soldier friend's yelled, "Finish it."

He turned back around and swung the whip in the air...smack—and a nail plunged into Jesus's shoulder blade. "Thirty-five, thirty-six, thirty-seven, thirty-eight."

A pause.

The crowd was still and quiet like Roman statues.

"Thirty-nine." That last blow knocked Jesus forward on the post almost taking oxygen out of his lungs.

The soldier lifted it again for one more strike at the back of Jesus, and then someone shouted and grabbed the soldier's hand and whip, "Enough. That is enough."

Jesus, the Messiah, went through a horrible beating for our healing. Words, plays and movies don't do justice in their attempt to depict what Jesus endured. He received stripes on his body for you and for me. With each blow a sickness was healed and hope was given for us to be whole. "For by his stripes we are healed."[41] It was His stripes for your healing and mine, and He suffered the pain, the disfigurement and torture *then* for us to have relief and healing *now*.

The stripes of Jesus can handle endometriosis and every other illness under heaven. While He received His stripes, He had me and you in mind, and knew we would face sickness in our bodies one day. He took one stripe for pain, another for cramps, another for cysts, another for cancer, another for AIDS, another for nerve damage, another for lupus, another for heart disease, and on and on. Whatever we will deal with...He suffered His stripes for us.

So, let us honor and receive the stripes of the Lord of heaven's armies today like a good soldier. A good soldier receives his or her stripes after a well-fought battle or tragedy they overcame. Well, Jesus not only endured the battle with sin, he endured a horrible Roman beating and a brutal Roman execution; then he came back to life and overcame death, hell and the grave. Hallelujah! All to save and to deliver the lost, to set the captives free, and to redeem us back to the Father. I'm trading my sickness for the healing that comes from His stripes. Who's with me?

Here's what I'm asking God...

God, I know Your word says, "By His (Jesus's) stripes we are healed." Cause this to be a reality in my life and body. Release to me a greater understanding by Your Spirit of the stripes of Jesus and the healing they bring. I believe by faith that by His stripes I am and was healed. Let healing manifest in my mind, body and soul. I declare I will walk in a greater depth of what the stripes of Jesus did for me.

Here's something to think on...

The Lord of Hosts and of heaven's armies received His stripes for your healing. (Isaiah 53:5).

Here's a tip to help you stand...

Cut thirty-nine strips of paper or fabric and create something to remind you of the stripes Jesus took for your healing. Create a cross using the strips, or a purse or a flag or badge and write on it your symptoms, illnesses, aches, pains, hurts and issues. Try making a thirty-nine striped collage. Be creative.

LETTER

Under His Wings

"Keep me as the apple of Your eye;
Hide me under the shadow of Your wings."
~King David (Psalm 17:8).

Dear *Woman*,

I hate creepy, damp, dark, cob-web infested basements. It's not the most pleasant place to be used as a place of safety. It can often be a more dangerous place sometimes than going out into the storm. But it's the go-to-place for severe weather like a tornado.

Have you ever been in a severe storm before? In a storm where there was a tornado warning and you had to take shelter? I remember participating in tornado drills in elementary school.

The school tornado alarm sounded at 9 a.m. blaring in my ear like an ambulance was driving down the hallway. It scared the living cells out of my body. Even though the teacher warned us, it still took me by surprise and sent my heart into doing jumping jacks in my chest. The exit lights flashed in the hallway like a photographer on the side of the runway.

Ms. Brown walked to the classroom door and spoke loud and slowly. "Okay class, this is a tornado drill. I want you to get up and walk slowly to the door and get in a single-file line." We scrambled out of our seats and made our way to the door. There I was staring at the back of a classmate's head.

"We're going to go out of this door and walk along the brick wall and down the gray stairs to the basement. Stay close to the wall," Ms. Brown said. Ah, the basement—it actually wasn't bad in schools since there were classes down there. But still it was a basement. And you already know my thoughts and feelings about basements. We made our way down the gray stairs to the ground level.

"Okay class, turn and face the wall and sit on the floor."

We turned and faced the wall and sat down on a hard, slick, icy-cold floor.

"Now fold your legs and put your head between your legs." Ms. Brown walked up and down the hallway to make sure our "safety" position was right. Oh, the days of being young and limber. The drill lasted for about ten minutes. Then it was over, and it was back to writing, reading, math, snacks and recess.

The tornado drills came, and they went. No damage and no one hurt. Well, I'm not in elementary school any more. And what I'm going through is not a pretend tornado drill that lasts for ten minutes—no it has been much longer. You and I have been through life's tornado storms, and they're real and sometimes difficult. I can't run to the basement to take cover and find safety from these storms, but I can run and take safety under the wings of God.

King David was familiar with taking cover and finding safety in God. He often wrote about taking shelter under the shadow of God's wings. God's wings were a place of peace, refuge and rest for David throughout his life.

His life was in danger several times, but one particular time was when he was on the run from the demonic King Saul, "his royal madness" (as I like to call him). He was so full of jealousy and hatred against his former apprentice and personal musician that he put a hit out against David. Everywhere he turned King Saul's soldiers were out to destroy him.

David didn't choose a basement for his safety. He hid in a cave once, but that wasn't his ultimate "go-to place" for safety. He took refuge under the wings of God, and that was his number-one hide-out spot for safety. David went into God's secret witness protection program, and no harm came to him at all. It was a secure, safe place. He stayed hidden under the shadow of God's wings until the death of King Saul and the rest of his enemies.

If the wings of God are good enough for King David, then they should be good enough for me, too, in the midst of my pain, cramps, nausea, trials, infertility, foreclosure, and sufferings. When life with endo-storms tries to hunt me down to take my life, passion, motivation, and joy, I run to safety under His wings with my legs folded and my face between my legs and pray. Unfortunately, I'm not as limber and flexible as I was back in elementary school.

Are you in the middle of a life-tornado storm? Are you experiencing severe trials, a heavy diagnosis, or 100 mph dangerous gusty situations? Are you on the run because something is hunting you down to kill your joy, to steal life from you and to destroy your passion and hope? What is your go-to-place for safety? Is it family, friends, or a spouse? Is it a church or a coffee house? Is it the nearest mall or bar or restaurant? Those places won't provide the ultimate safety that we need in the midst of our severe storms. Take cover under the shadow of His wings like David.

We can rest and stay there under His wings for however long we want and need to. We will be safe there. We will be sound there. We will be secure there. And whatever is hunting us down will soon die, and we will be delivered from all our enemies because *God Almighty is our safety.*

Here's what I'm asking God...

God, let my joy come like the morning sun after a storm. I take cover under the shadow of Your wings. I will rest and remain there until the storms pass. Nothing can penetrate your protection over me. And I will trust in the shelter of Your wings. I declare joy will arrive in my morning time. (Psalm 30:5).

Here's something to think on...

Hiding under God's wings is better than hiding in a basement or cave any day. (Psalm 91:4).

Here's a tip to help you stand...

Get to your hideout spot (the Wings of God) and get in your safety position: whether it be the good ol' fashioned legs folded with your head between your legs. Or bowing down in prayer, or relaxing with your feet propped up on a pillow, or laying on the floor or bed, or sitting straight up.

Whatever your safety position is, stay covered under His wings, and you will be safe.

LETTER 35

You're on His Mind

> "What is man that You are mindful of him,
> And the son of man that You visit him?"
> ~David (Psalm 8:4).

Dear *Woman*,

Have you ever thought about someone, a friend or family member, and that very day or the next day you saw them, or they called or sent you a text? This happens to me all the time. It's crazy how that happens. You were mindful of that person. Your thoughts were about them.

Have you ever thought about God, the Creator of the Universe, thinking about you? Did you know His thoughts are full of you? Yes, you. Every day. Before the foundations of the world, when He placed you in your mother's womb.

He's thinking of you this very moment. The Lord is mindful of you and me. David said, "What is man that You are mindful of him and the son of man that You should visit him? You made him a little lower than the angels." (Psalm 8:4-5).

What an honor to have the God of the Universe thinking of me! Thinking of you. Thinking of mankind whom He created and formed into walking, breathing, dust humans.

You are on His mind. You might not always know what He's thinking, but you can trust that His thoughts are positive. He doesn't hate you or think evil toward you. They're good. He's thinking the best about you. "For I know the thoughts that I think toward you, says the Lord, thoughts of peace and not of evil, to give you a future and a hope." (Jeremiah 29:11). He doesn't take joy in your suffering or pain. He is our High Priest who sympathizes with our weakness and is familiar with suffering. He is well acquainted with pain. He doesn't run out of good thoughts about you. You are not an afterthought.

He's mindful of our destiny. He is mindful of our condition and the days lying in the bed or on the couch unable to function. He is mindful of your trips to doctors' appointments, your treatments and medications. He's thinking of you, and you're not forgotten, but forever before Him. You are written on the palm of His hand.[42]

His thoughts of you outnumber the grains of sand on the shore. Our good God has good thoughts about you, His daughter. He's concerned, considerate, aware, alert and knowledgeable even when life experiences and situations try to tell us, "Hey, you know that God you believe in? He's not even thinking about you."

But the truth is, God is thinking of you and me. God is so into us, and He can't help but think about you. Let's declare the words of this song:

> *"God's thoughts of me are many*
> *God's thoughts of me are good*
> *God's thoughts of me outnumber the sand on the shore*
>
> *He can't forget me*
> *He won't forget me*
> *God is mindful of me."*[43]

We occupy the mind of God, and there is nothing that can evict us from His mind.

You're on His Mind

Here's what I'm asking God...

God, You are a mindful God, very concerned and considerate. Remember your handmaiden in the times of my greatest need and desires. Your thoughts are not like my thoughts nor Your ways like my ways, for they're higher than mine.[44] I want to know Your thoughts about me. I'm honored to know I'm on your mind this very moment. I declare God's thoughts are kind, sweet and pleasant toward me, my family and my destiny.

Here's something to think on...

His thoughts about you are uncountable. (Psalm 139:17-18).

Here's a tip to help you stand...

I dare you to ask God this question, "What do you think about me? What are your thoughts of me? Wait and listen and write what He speaks to you. It will encourage your heart.

V. Woman Thou Art Loosed

LETTER 36

Friends of Faith

"As iron sharpens iron, So a man sharpens the countenance of his friend."
~King Solomon (Proverbs 27:17).

Dear *Woman*,

I hit a gold rush—a gold rush in friends, that is. Good friends are a special treasure to find and to have. I'm sure you're one of those good friends that is a rare find or maybe you have one or two of those in your life. If good friends are a rare find and a treasure, then what are friends that are full of faith for you?

To me, friends of faith are a kiss from God.

In Mark 9, there was a paralyzed man, who experienced this kind of friendship. He was carried by four men. The Bible doesn't say if they were his friends or not, but I assume they were his friends (they could've been his family). Let's imagine they were his friends.

These four men carried the paralyzed man to Peter's house and tore a hole in the roof because the house was packed with a large crowd. They were determined to get him in front of Jesus. They didn't let the obstacle of the large crowd stop them. They were creative, innovative and full of faith to get this man to Jesus so their friend could be healed. And because of the faith of these four men, Jesus healed the paralyzed man.

The chapter didn't say anything about this man's faith. But Jesus saw their faith, and it moved Him to act on behalf of that man.

How is your faith for your friend dealing with cancer, lupus or another illness or infertility or unemployment or a prodigal child or a broken marriage on the verge of divorce? What will your faith do for them? What will your friends' faith do for you?

God gave me a big fat kiss and a gold rush called "friends of faith" (FoFs). I joined the staff of an international ministry that has made a great impact in my life for over twelve years. After being in this ministry for about a year, I couldn't hide my illness anymore. I finally opened up and shared with these women, who were now my close friends, about this "silent disease" and what I went through on a monthly basis during my periods.

My friends said, "We're going to begin to pray for you about this. The enemy can't do this to you. The pattern will be broken." To hear those words was huge to me because up until that time, I felt alone except for the support of my husband, my mother and my sister. They would pray for me each month, and I'm so appreciative of them. But outside of my family, I had never experienced this level of support, love, kindness, compassion, and faith.

Now God brought friends of faith (FoFs) into my life from that ministry and a few from outside of that ministry to stand with me. There were times I reached out to a few of my FoFs via text, "I need prayer; my period is about to start, and I need grace and peace and strength to endure for the next couple of days. Thank you."

My phone buzzed immediately with replies of, "Will do, praying for you, and sure will." And some would even text a prayer to me. They became my support system—my period buddies. With their support I received strength to endure those times of the month.

I wasn't alone anymore; I had warrior friends armed with faith fighting with me. There's a popular verse in the Bible (Ecclesiastes 4:9, 12 NLT) that says: "Two people are better than one, for they can help each other succeed. A person standing alone can be attacked and defeated, but two can stand back-to-back and conquer. Three are even better, for a triple-braided cord is not easily broken." I wonder, what can five or ten do?

One month, I sent a text to ten women to pray for me so I would endure the endo-storm, and I felt their prayers. There's real power, victory, and strength in numbers.

Even though I knew my FoFs loved and cared for me without any judgment, somehow shame chimed in: "You shouldn't send a text this month. They're probably getting tired of you asking them to pray for you over this same issue. Just fight it on your own." So I wouldn't send out a text at all, and guess what, I noticed the difference when I didn't text them. I know those thoughts aren't true, but sometimes it felt wrong or selfish to keep asking for prayer for the same issue.

I know good friends—especially FoFs—don't think that way. One friend recently told me, "Chavos, will you please send me a text during those times so I can pray?" Her words meant a lot to me and shattered the thoughts: "They're getting tired of praying for you."

My friends of faith carried me (like the paralyzed man's friends did for him) not literally, but in the spirit, in prayer to the throne of God. It doesn't matter what they see or hear month after month. They remain in faith and in prayer that God will heal me one day. Their confident, relentless attitude, and response to bad reports is, "We are going to conquer this thing!"

Friends join in with each other's struggles, so it's no longer "I" but "we." Wow, I am the richest gal in the world. God gave me a great treasure and gold rush of friends of faith. I'm not special. If God did it for me, He can do it for you, too.

Maybe you're reading this, and you don't have what this man had or what I've talked about. There's hope. I believe God wants to release friends of faith (FoFs) to you. Along my journey I had to be vulnerable, open and transparent and not afraid to ask for prayer, help and support to be able to receive from my FoFs.

Maybe some of you experienced friends like Job, who thought you'd sinned and that's why you're dealing with your current situation. Job said: "My friends scorn me; my eyes pour out tears to God. My relatives have failed, and my close friends have forgotten me." (Job 16:20, 19:14). Do you feel like this? I'm sorry you've experienced this kind of so-called friendship; this is not what God wants for you.

There are people that care and understand what you're dealing with and who can relate to you. Be of good cheer, friends of faith (FoFs) are coming to you, and they are full of faith, love, compassion and hope for you. Most of all, we can always rely on the greatest Friend of all friends, one who will stick closer than any brother.

> *"Oh, what a friend we have in Jesus,*
> *All our sins and griefs to bear!*
>
> *Can we find a friend so faithful*
> *Who will all our sorrows share?*
> *Jesus knows our every weakness*
> *Take it to the Lord in prayer.*
>
> *Do your friends despise and forsake you?*
> *Take it to the Lord in prayer!*
> *In His arms He'll take and shield you*
> *You will find a solace there."* [45]
> *(song by Joseph Scriven)*

Here's what I'm asking God...

God, bring true friends of faith into my life that I trust and who have hearts of understanding and compassion. Reveal them to me, and let my heart be open to whatever way you send them. A friend is one who loves at all times. I want this type of friendship, and let me be this kind of friend to others. Thank you for releasing a gold rush of friends into my life for this season. Thank you for their faith, love and support. They are a rare gem and a kiss from You, God. Bless and encourage them. Most of all, I'm grateful for Your friendship, You are a friend who sticks closer than a brother. I declare I am not alone. I have friends because I show myself friendly, and I have godly friendships in the spirit.

Here's something to think on...

A friend stays close and is always ready to love—in the good and bad times. (Proverbs 17:17; 18:24).

Here's a tip to help you stand...

Ask God for friends of faith (FoFs): Who around you is full of faith, love and compassion? Are they in your church, work, school or women's group? Is it your spouse or sister or mother or a friend? Can you be open, transparent and honest with them in this season of your life? Create a support group from those friends and ask them if they would be willing to pray and encourage you when needed. Don't be afraid to open up to them. We need each other.

I would love to be a part of your "friends of faith," please don't hesitate to contact me. (See the back of this book.) Looking forward to hearing from you soon, Friend.

LETTER 37

He Touched Me

"...Your strong right hand holds me securely."
~David (Psalm 63:8 NLT).

Dear *Woman*,

"He touched me, Oh He touched me. And oh the joy that floods my soul. Something happened, and now I know. He touched me and made me whole. He touched me and made me whole."[46] I imagine our "*dear woman*" friend (in Luke 13) bursting out in this song after Jesus touched her.

Her life was changed forever from just one touch. Her eighteen-year-long battle with the spirit of infirmity was gone, done and over, from just one touch. Her crippled posture was made straight, from just one touch. Not just any touch and not by any hands, but from the hands that would soon be nailed to the cross. Those hands reached out and touched her.

I heard it said that, "Human touch can aid in pain relief, stress and anxiety reduction, and even lower blood pressure when it's done in a non-sexual but soothing way. It can bring about healing to the body." Some of us may have experienced this through massages or chiropractic treatment.

Wow, if this statement is true about the human touch, and it does all of that, how much more will the God touch do. Human touch is so limited and might help relieve pain for a while, and we have to keep going back, but one touch from the hand of God, and it's all done.

Jesus healed people in so many different ways. Some people He spoke the word to. Others—He asked them what they wanted Him to do. One woman touched His garment, and others He touched.

There is power in His touch. His touch causes crooked things to be straight. His touch produces results—deliverance.

The Lord's hand is mighty. He delivered the children of Israel out of the land of Egypt with a mighty hand. If He did that for them after hearing their cries, He will surely do the same for you and me and bring us out of the land of infirmity and affliction by His mighty hand. Who can stop His hand from acting on my behalf? Who can climb up to Heaven and handcuff the hands of Almighty God? No one. All power is in His hands.

The right hand of God is mentioned a lot in scripture:

"The right hand of the Lord is exalted; The right hand of the Lord does valiantly." (Psalm 118:16).

"His right hand and His holy arm have gained Him the victory." (Psalm 98:1).

"Powerful is your arm! Strong is your hand! Your right hand is lifted high in glorious strength." (Psalm 89:13 NLT).

"Your right hand, O LORD, is glorious in power. Your right hand, O LORD, smashes the enemy." (Exodus 15:6 NLT).

The hand of the Lord repairs and heals. The hand of the Lord shall be known to His servants.[47]

If His servants took the stand and testified about how His touch healed and restored them and did great things in their lives, I imagine they would say:

"He touched me and made my womb come alive and caused me to give birth to a son at an old age," Sarah testifies.

"He touched my lips with coals from the altar and sent me as a messenger," Isaiah testifies.

"He touched me and extended my life for another fifteen years," Hezekiah testifies.

"He touched me, and though I once was blind, now I see," the former blind man testifies.

"He touched me, and now I can worship with my guitar, pain-free," my friend Marcy would testify.

"He touched me and healed me from cancer," another friend would testify.

What will you testify? What will be our testimony about His touch? I want to be able to say, "He touched me, and all the endometriosis in my body and all the fibroids dried up, and now I'm healed and free." I long for His touch and for His hand to be strong upon me and you. And when His hand is strong upon us, it will repair, heal, strengthen, cure, hold, encourage, help and aid us. We can't see His hand upon us, but we can be confident that He upholds us by His right hand. And by His touch all will be well.

Here's what I'm asking God...

God, I need a touch from You. Let me feel Your touch. Stretch out Your mighty hand and heal me. For Your right hand is strong and powerful. Your right hand and Your holy arm have gained You the victory. I declare the Lord's hand is strong upon me to cure, repair, strengthen, hold, encourage and help me.

Here's something to think on...

God's hands aren't and can't be handcuffed from rescuing you. (Psalm 20:6).

Here's a tip to help you stand...

Listen to the song, "*He Touched Me*" on YouTube and journal about His touch, and write out a hope list of what you want His touch to do in your life, body, and family. Do a study on the hand of the Lord.

LETTER 38

Loose Me and Let Me Go

> "But when Jesus saw her, He called her to Him and said to her, "Woman, you are loosed from your infirmity."
> ~Luke (Luke 13:12).

Dear *Woman*,

Our friend (in Luke 13) was free now. Free to do whatever she wanted to do. Free to accomplish dreams she had set aside for eighteen years. Free to go places she always wanted to visit.

As she walked in the marketplace square, people whispered, "Is she the one that was in captivity by a spirit of infirmity for eighteen years? She's free now."

She turned back with a smile on her face and answered, "Yes, I am the one. No pain and no bondage. Rabbi Jesus, declared to me, 'Woman you are loosed from your infirmity.' I'm a free woman."

There were no more limitations and restrictions. Before, she could only do certain things, limited in what she could do and where she could go. Not anymore. She became a free woman, released from an eighteen-year-long prison sentence. She had to renew her mind and remind herself she was no longer in captivity but a loosed woman.

Whenever her thoughts or actions resembled her old, captive behavior, she declared and sang about her freedom,

> *"There's no more chains holding me*
> *There's no more pain restricting me*

> *The Son of God has set me free*
> *The Son of God has ransomed me*
> *The Son of God loves me*
>
> *I am free, free to be*
> *I am free, free indeed*
> *I am free, free to be.*"[48]

There was someone else loosed from their captivity, who might be inclined to sing this same song. His name was Lazarus. Lazarus died and was in the grave for four days before Jesus came to the tomb to release him from his captivity. (See John 11.)

Jesus called, "Lazarus, come forth."[49]

Lazarus came forth with his hands and feet bound and his whole body totally wrapped up.

Jesus called to those around him, "Loose him, and let him go."[50]

Our *"dear woman"* friend and Lazarus have similar, yet different stories of captivity. She was bound on the inside, and he was bound on the outside. Both were loosed from the thing that restricted movement in their lives and ceased their forward progress. Jesus came and loosed them in two different ways. He touched and spoke to the woman, and He told others to loose Lazarus.

There are three ways we are loosed from things in our life: by God, by others and by shaking ourselves free. I love the verse in Isaiah 52:2:

> "Shake yourself from the dust, arise; Sit down, O Jerusalem!
> Loose yourself from the bonds of your neck, O captive daughter of Zion!"

The time came for their release from captivity, and so it shall for me and you. I will arise and shake myself loose and declare, "Loose me, and let me go, endo!" It doesn't have a right to be in my body. It doesn't belong there. "Let go, endo. You can no longer hold my womb, intestines or any other organs captive. Let go, endo. You don't have a right to my body." My declaration is let go, endo and whatever else would try to hold me back. It's time for freedom and release in my life and body.

The time has come for you to be released, too. Be loosed. Be free. Freedom is coming to you like the "*dear woman*" and Lazarus. He speaks over you and over me, "Woman, you are loosed from your infirmity." And may we sing, declare and pray: "No more suffering, no more symptoms, no more pain, no more bleeding. I'm free to be. No longer restricted to the bed, couch, hospital, or limitations in what I can or cannot do."

Some of you have been dealing with a sickness, an addiction, depression, disorders in your body for such a long time that you stopped counting. It's time to be released. For some of you it's been a short time, and it's time for you, too. It's time to be loosed. The handcuffs of the illness must be unlocked from around my womb. So, the handcuffs of your illness, too (cancer, fibromyalgia, lupus, heart disease, PCOS) must be unlocked from your body.

What will you declare? Will it be:

- Loose me and let me go Cancer!
- Loose me and let me go anxiety disorder.
- Loose me and let me go depression.
- Loose me and let me go anger.

I hear the prison doors opening and the sirens sounding; there's a mass JAILBREAK taking place!

Here's what I'm asking God...

God, I desire to be loosed from sickness, depression, disorders, (name your thing). Let Your word go forth from Your mouth and accomplish and produce fruit in my life. Speak the words, 'Woman you are loosed' over me, and I will be loosed. I declare, let go endo (name your illness or issue), you must release me.

Here's something to think on...

God himself will loose you, command others to loose you and grace you to loose yourself. (Isaiah 52:2; John 11:44).

Here's a tip to help you stand...

Arise and shake yourself loose. Do a study on the word "loose" (I like to use the Blue Letter Bible website, but you can use whatever source you like.) Define and describe this: What does being "loosed" look like to you?

LETTER 39

Rest a While

"Oh, that I had wings like a dove! I would fly away and be at rest."
~David (Psalm 55:6).

Dear *Woman*,

I sleep like a cat. So I've been told by my beloved husband. I admit, I do like to rest any chance I get. Maybe a little too much at times. There's nothing wrong with resting. You have to fight for rest these days. Especially in our society where everything is fast paced. For example, as soon as you get a new phone or tablet, it is already outdated.

We are a Facebook and Twitter generation, on the go and in the know. Checking our email every minute or reading blog after blog. I'm guilty of this. It's good to take some time to rest and not feel like I always have to be doing something. It's okay to just pause and rest. Have you been able to rest lately?

The Good Shepherd of our souls will lead us beside still waters.[51] He directs our steps and shows us how to rest because we've been through trials and sufferings that have made some of us weary, tired and worn. Some of us have experienced tumultuous and boisterous waters. Others have experienced fast rushing floodwaters that almost overtook us. Some of you have experienced deep waters that have come to your ankles, then your knees, your waist, all the way to your neck and almost covered your head. King David understands about deep waters. He wrote,

> "Save me, O God, for the floodwaters are up to my neck. Deeper and deeper I sink into the mire; I can't find a foothold. I am in deep water, and the floods overwhelm me." (Psalm 69:1-2 NLT).

He asked God, "Pull me from these deep waters. Don't let the floods overwhelm me, or the deep waters swallow me." (Psalm 69:14-15).

God will pull us from deep waters and not allow the floods to overwhelm us. He leads us beside still waters. You and I will enter a season of still waters. Can you hear the still waters? Probably not, they don't make a lot of noise. You're going from a season where there's a lot of noise, distractions, busyness and loud clutter that drains the joy, peace, and creativity of life out of you into a season of quietness. Sometimes my own thoughts have been noise; other people's thoughts and opinions can be noise. To go from a place of noise to silence can be a shock to my system.

Stillness and silence can be awkward at times because they leave us with our thoughts, feelings and things that we haven't wanted to face or deal with. We can no longer ignore those things when the noise is on mute. It confuses the performance-driven, busy, keep-it-moving-and-going attitude and mind. Stillness causes us to go at the pace of a snail in a cheetah world.

He causes us to lie down in green pastures to rest in a fruitful and beautiful place, where there is life and growth.[52] He will restore, revive and refresh our souls. Springtime is coming for you and me, who've been in a dry, barren, lifeless, hard winter season.

Picture yourself laying in an open lush field with the wind blowing upon your face, causing the fresh smell of new blades of grass to tickle your nose. You hear the sound of the birds, "chirp, chirp" from a nearby oak tree. You've embraced the previous season of loud noise and fruitlessness well in a posture of faith and trust, and now it's time to enter this new season of springtime.

The Good Shepherd is saying to us, "Come my child and rest a while in this place and partake of the still waters, not the loud and boisterous waters like you've experienced. Be restored and refreshed for the journey ahead. Enjoy times of sweet fellowship with the Holy Spirit. Rest beside the still waters, do nothing at all but rest, take a cat nap; it's okay, just be still and know that I am God."

Here's what I'm asking God...

God, You are my Good Shepherd, and I will follow You to the still waters, to the way of rest. Cause me to lie down in a fruitful place of green pastures and take me from the wintery, dry barren season. Restore and refresh my soul, my mind and my spirit. I declare I will be still and know that You are God and springtime has come.

Here's something to think on...

God is your life *savior*, and he will keep you from drowning in deep waters. (Isaiah 43:2).

Here's a tip to help you stand...

Get your spring clothes ready. Follow the Good Shepherd, and take a cat nap by the still waters.

LETTER 40

Peace, Be Still

> "God cannot give us a happiness and peace apart from Himself, because it is not there. There is no such thing."[53]
>
> ~C.S. Lewis

Dear *Woman*,

If it's not one storm, it's another. Have you felt like this? The disciples probably felt like this, too. The disciples were in two different storms during their time with Jesus (at least that is what is written in the Bible. It could've been more, but we're not told). They were fishermen made for the waves and storms, but you wouldn't know it by their reactions to the storms they experienced.

During one storm, Jesus was in the boat with them, and he declared, "Peace, be still." And the weather had to obey his voice. Afterwards He asked the disciples, "Where is your faith?" (see Mark 4:39-40).

The second storm, Jesus wasn't on the boat with them, but he saw what they were experiencing from a distance. He came to them walking on the water and stepped into their boat, and the wind immediately stopped its forceful blowing, whirling and whistling (see Matthew 14:25).

The disciples worshiped him saying, "Truly you are the Son of God." [54]

The disciples' response after each storm was different. The first storm, they said, "Who can this be? For He commands even the winds and water, and they obey Him!"[55] And the second storm, it was settled in their hearts about who He was.

Our storms reveal God to us in a way we never would've seen him if we hadn't gone through the pain. Our storms invite us to experience a greater revelation of the miraculous working power of God. After our storms, our response will be like the disciples'. We will worship and proclaim, "Truly you are the Son of God." We will *know* that we *know* God and his character after it's all over. If we can just hold on in the midst of the chaos, struggles, trials and storms, we will gain a deeper knowledge of God.

Peace is needed the most when there is chaos. At times, in the midst of the chaotic cycles in my life a peace would cover my entire body like a blanket, and I'd snuggle under it and rest. I'd cry to God like a child scared of a monster under my bed, and God would come and comfort me with His peace. I don't fully understand it, but I've felt the peace of God more during my endo-storms than during the clear and sunny days. I guess, that's His peace that surpasses understanding. Those were special times when the Prince of Peace visited me.

Are you in the middle of a storm, challenge or difficult situation? Do they seem to come back to back? Your stomach might feel like a big ocean on the inside, and your food or liquid wants to ride the waves. I speak peace to your stomach. Your mind might be full of worry, doubt and uncertainty. Peace to your mind and soul. You might be in excruciating pain, and it feels like 5000 tons is sitting on your abdomen. Peace to your body.

He knows you're experiencing these storms. I know He might seem distant and far off in another country or land. But He's aware and will come and step into your boat (life). He comes as the *Prince of Peace* today to give you peace—peace which surpasses what you're experiencing. Peace which surpasses what you're feeling. Peace which surpasses what you're thinking.

He declares over your storm, pain, and shame, "Peace, be still." And the wind, whirlwinds, rain, thunder and lightning cease.

He speaks, "Peace, be still" to our minds and bodies. "Peace, be still cramping. Be still dysmenorrhea. Peace, be still abdominal pain. Be still, fatigue, dizziness, bloating and headaches. Peace, be still heavy flowing menorrhagia. Be still nausea, diarrhea and constipation. Peace, be still dehydration. Be still discouragement, anger, sadness and depression. Peace, be still cancer cells. Be still to your joints, bones and legs. Peace, be still immune system. Peace, be still, my daughter for I am God—The God of Peace."

And because He is God and everything must obey His voice, this will be our declaration, "When peace like a river attends my way, like sorrows and sea bellows roll, whatever my lot, thou hast taught me to say, it is well, it is well with my soul." [56]

Here's what I'm asking God...

God, all creation obeys you. Even the winds and the waves obey your voice, and the symptoms (name your symptoms) I'm experiencing in my body must obey your voice, too. Will You speak to the storms in my life, my body, my mind and my heart and let Your peace cover me? You will keep me in perfect peace for my mind is stayed on You, because I trust in You. (Isaiah 26:3). I declare the Prince of Peace rests and abides inside of me continually.

Here's something to think on...

God's peace is a guard. (Philippians 4:6-7).

Here's a tip to help you stand...

Speak to your storm: say it out loud, scream it or whisper it, "Peace, Be Still" and believe it will obey your voice because the Prince of Peace lives on the inside of you.

LETTER 41

Punk Your Period

> "By this I know that You are well pleased with me, because my enemy does not triumph over me."
> ~David (Psalm 41:11).

Dear *Woman*,

I'm a bully. I know, shame on me, right? But first hear me out. I don't bully people like Shauna Brown; I bully my body and my period, which has bullied me for years. Who is Shauna Brown? She's a childhood classmate my mom will never forget. Here's the story.

It was Bree's (my mom) 8th grade year in 1973. She was a smart straight A student. And besides just having brains, she had the looks, too. She was 5'5" slender, with brown skin, beautiful dark-drown eyes, and long black hair that flowed down her back, and she was a fashionable dresser. Her combination of brains and beauty incited anger, envy and jealousy in some of the girls in her junior high school. It also didn't make for a peaceful school environment. It was hostile.

There was a girl, who was the leader of the pack of "mean girls," named Shauna. She was 5'3" light-skin, a broader build with short sandy brownish hair. She was overcome with envy and jealousy. She absolutely hated my mother and made sure to bully, tease and intimidate her every day before and after classes. "Girl, what do you have on today? Did your mama buy that from the thrift store?"

It's like she woke up with a mission to bully Bree. Bree endured her insulting comments and constant taunting. She angrily clutched her books tightly and quickly made her way to her classroom. She slammed the door behind her and walked to her favorite steel desk by the window and flopped down in her seat. "I'm so angry and tired of Shauna's comments. She waits to bully me every day," she said to herself.

After the bell rang for lunch, Bree quickly gathered her class books and her purple notebook and hurried to put them in her silver locker. She dialed her combination lock and swung open the locker.

"Well, looky here," Shauna yelled from down the hall. "If it isn't miss skinny minnie."

Bree looked straight ahead into her neatly organized locker with books in order. Fury came over her, and she slammed her locker and closed the lock, "Look Shauna, you better back off, okay. I've had enough of your mouth."

"What you say to me, girl?" Shauna said, now all in Bree's face.

Ms. Johnson, the math teacher, looked outside her classroom and asked, "Is everything okay, girls?"

The mean girl crew all sang in unison, "Yes, Ms. Johnson."

"Okay, hurry to lunch now," Ms. Johnson said returning to her classroom.

Shauna leaned over and whispered to Bree, "I'll meet you after school."

Hours later the school bell rang, and another school day ended. Students rushed out of their classrooms all at once like a synchronized rodeo with doors flinging open. Everyone ran out to get to their buses. The once quiet hallway was now filled with "'see ya tomorrows', 'byes' and 'hey whatcha doing tonights?' 'Want to study together at the library?'"

Bree slowly walked down the noise-filled hallway with dread-filled steps to meet Shauna. After her fearful inspection en route to her bus, there was no Shauna. She didn't meet Bree after school at all.

"Hmmm, maybe she forgot." Bree sprinted to the yellow school bus. The ride home was like any other day and was filled with thoughts about Shauna's bullying; her words soaked deep into Bree's mind and heart. She replayed the day over and over and was so engulfed in her thoughts she didn't realize the bus was in front of her house.

"Bree, Bree, here's your stop," the bus driver yelled.

Bree jumped up and grabbed her backpack. "Sorry, Mr. Sam. Thank you, and have a good day," she said as she jumped off the bus.

Bree entered the house and threw her bag on the couch. Greeted by the sweet voice of her mother coming from the kitchen, "Bree, how was school today?"

"It was okay. Class was fun, but Shauna is still saying things to me, and today I said something back to her." Bree walked towards the kitchen and leaned against a wall.

"Bree, I told you to quit saying things back to her. Go about your way."

"Mom, that's hard to do every day," Bree said with tears in her eyes.

Her mother grabbed butter from the fridge and advised, "You can't argue with someone if they're quiet."

Bree knew what her mother said was right, but she knew it wouldn't be easy. "What if Shauna thinks I'm scared of her," she thought.

Bree took her mother's advice, though difficult, and decided not to say anything back to Shauna. Day after day, Shauna hurled her taunts, insults and intimidating actions at Bree. However, Bree was quiet and didn't say one word back to Shauna.

One day Shauna was up to her usual bullying ways, "Girl, what you wearing today? Some thrift store special your mama got you."

Bree ignored her and kept on walking to her classroom with her books in one hand and her favorite yellow and white polka dot umbrella in the other.

"Girl, I know you heard me." Shauna stepped in front of Bree's path and said, "I'm tired of looking at your ugly face day after day. I'm going to beat you up right now."

Bree didn't say one thing to her, she kept her head and feet straight forward. Shauna grabbed her arm, "Girl, did you hear me? I said, bring it!"

Bree snatched her arm away from Shauna and swung her yellow and white polka dot umbrella around and bushwhacked Shauna right in the face.

Shauna grabbed her face and fell on the ground in pain and shock. And that was the last time Shauna ever bullied Bree. There was no more, "Girl, this and girl that," or "I'll meet you after school."

I'm not condoning violence, but I'm happy my mother stood up for herself.

For years I allowed my period to bully me month after month and year after year. It would scream, "You better lay down and stay down because as soon as you get up you know what I will do to you. Don't laugh or speak to anyone. You better give me all your energy and attention." I let the bullying go on far too long, and I was done bowing down under the weight of my period. I turned on my period like a street light turns to green, and I punked (put it in check) my period. Sometimes it won, but I would come back with a fight.

I stood up for myself like my mother did to her bully and reminded my period who's the boss. I was no longer going to listen to its threats and intimidating words anymore. One way I showed it that I was its master was by physical activity. I'd talk and walk, which were two very difficult tasks in my condition. Step by step and word by word, I was punking my period and endo. It would back down and behave for a while and sometimes it would retaliate, but I didn't care because its bullying tactics were powerless.

If you get bullied long enough you turn and get even and deal with it. Shauna would tease my mom, and talk about her every day. Until one day, my mother took that umbrella...and the rest is history. The bully never messed with her again.

Don't you think it's time for you to stand up and deal with that illness, depression, negative talk and discouraging words or whatever that "thing" is that's bullied and tormented you for such a long time. God promises us that "No weapon formed against us will prosper, and every tongue that rises up against us in judgment we will condemn." (Isaiah 54:17). He's given us the power to condemn (show to be in the wrong) those things that speak against us. We're called to be bold as a lion, courageous, fearless and exerting our authority and dominion in the Kingdom of God.

Here's what I'm asking God...

God, make me bold as a lion to confront tormenting and intimidating thoughts. You said you have given me power over the serpents, scorpions and over all the power of the enemy. Cause me to walk in that power and not bow down or cower to the bullying of the enemy, pain, my periods or any other thing that may try to oppress me. I will be bold and courageous in You, my God. I declare no weapon formed against me will prosper, and anything that rises up against me to speak negative to me I will condemn. (Isaiah 54:17).

Here's something to think on...

You're a master, and your body is your slave. (1 Corinthians 9:27 NIV).

Here's a tip to help you stand...

One way I punk my period is to go for a walk. Your way might look completely different due to physical restraints. But think of a way to punk your period or your fears or your depression, etc. Buy a yellow polka dot umbrella or whatever color you desire and use it as a reminder to show your period, sickness, fear, depression, doubt, trial...who you are: You're its master, and you won't be bullied by it.

LETTER 42

Stand Up Straight

> "Stand up and bless the Lord your God forever and ever!"
> ~The Levites (Nehemiah 9:5).

Dear *Woman*,

Have you ever been told to stand up or sit up straight? Don't slouch, but stand up tall? Oh, how I hated to hear that from my teachers. It felt more comfortable and took less energy to slouch than to position myself in the shape of a L with my back pressed against the hard wooden desk chair. Even though I hated hearing "sit up straight," I did feel different. I felt more alert and had the strength to fight going to dreamland. I'm sure my posture changed how I looked, too.

Our "*dear woman*" friend (in Luke 13) had a slouching, bent over position, not because she wanted to hang out and relax or because she wasn't interested in the teaching in the synagogue. Her condition caused her to be in this unfavorable and uncomfortable position. She was bent over, cast down and crushed under the weight of her sickness. I wonder if she was depressed and oppressed in her soul.

People probably looked at her and thought, "She needs to stand up and sit up straight and not slouch, and it would help her posture. It'd help her feel better." But little did they know or maybe they did know, her bent position wasn't done on purpose. Her unwanted slouching posture was about to change before their eyes.

She thought she was going to the synagogue to hear a great teaching by Rabbi Jesus. The synagogue was about to be turned into a doctor's office, and that Jewish Rabbi (aka The Great Physician) was going to do chiropractic therapy and adjustments to her body.

He will do the same in my body and yours, and not only in our bodies but in our minds, souls and spirits, too. When Jesus got finished with her, she was positioned upright. She went from a 45-degree posture to a 90-degree posture, a perfect posture. She looked taller and probably felt better to be able to stand up straight and look at people face to face. She wasn't just standing up straight on the outside, but on the inside, too.

I'm in need of spiritual chiropractic therapy. I need to be adjusted. How about you? No more bent over or slouching posture. No more sad, down and depressed days. No more head bent down with eyes to the floor and heart broken in pieces. No more weights of worry, anxiety and stress altering my stance.

Let's get on the table, lay in the bed or on the floor and allow Jesus, *the Great Physician*, to make the needed chiropractic adjustments. He will change our posture and position and give us a powerful stance. So, don't be afraid if you hear some cracking, snapping and popping; this will be for your good.

You and I are called to be women of honor and stature. We're confident and unafraid to share our struggles, sufferings, pain, failures, successes and victories. Let's stand up tall in our identity. Stand up straight in our purpose. Stand up straight with confidence. Stand up straight as a woman on a mission. Stand up for the rights of others.

We will stand up straight and tall, facing the world eye to eye with our shoulders back, stomachs in, necks elongated and heads held high. We will know that God is the lifter of our heads.[57]

Stand Up Straight

Here's what I'm asking God...

God, give me strength and the power and grace to stand. Remove all hindrances and restrictions that would cause me to be bent over, oppressed, depressed, dejected, sad and weighed down. Come and do spiritual chiropractic therapy and adjustments in my body and life that I may stand up tall like a daughter of the King. Rise up and stand inside of me, Lord. I declare my back is strong, my faith is strong and my confidence is strong. And having done all, I will stand and see this great thing which the Lord will do before my eyes. (Ephesians 6:10; 1 Samuel 12:16).

Here's something to think on...

The Great Physician (the Lord) makes crooked places straight.
(Isaiah 42:16; 45:2).

Here's a tip to help you stand...

Standing up straight looks good on you; put on the shoes of peace and stand. Stand by sharing your story; stand by forming a support group. Stand by writing a blog post. Stand by taking a small step toward your purpose and dream today. Stand by treating yourself to a massage or chiropractic adjustment if doctor approved. Whatever you do - Stand!

LETTER 43

Praise Is What I Do

"I will bless the Lord at all times; his praise shall continually be in my mouth."
~David (Psalm 34:1).

Dear *Woman*,

Praise is what I do even when I'm going through. No, not really...not all the time. It's such a challenge praising God when I'm going through. How about you? I love praising God when it's easy, no challenges, no pain and no worries. I stand with hands lifted up and sing, "Praise is what I do, even when I'm going through. I lift my hands in praise. And I vow to praise You through the good and the bad. I'll praise You, whether happy or sad. I'll praise You in all that I go through, because praise is what I do. Cause I owe it all to you."[58]

You know, I've sung that popular song by William Murray, so many times during worship without any real understanding of the words to that song, until my journey with endo. I was now confronted with those words "I vow to praise you through the good and the bad. I praise you whether happy or sad." I had no idea I was really making a vow to God when I sang those words. I guess I need to be careful what I sing, huh. Now, in the midst of my going through, my vow was due.

David said, "Vows made to You are binding upon me, O God; I will render praises to You." (Psalm 56:12).

It's so much easier to praise God when everything is okay, but not that easy when I don't feel well. It takes more effort and sacrifice to praise him. It didn't happen all the time during endo episodes, but there were times I would lift up my weak voice in song and raise my heavy hands standing or sitting. I pushed through to praise him while I was going through.

One great example for me of someone praising God in the midst of going through is my friend Marcy—5'7", blonde hair, sweet, fun, anointed psalmist, song writer, wife, mother, and lover of God.

She leads and enjoys times of praise and worship with her guitar. But there was a time this all stopped. In September 2011, Marcy experienced stiffness in her neck for about a week. She "rolled over in bed one morning and was immediately in excruciating pain." She didn't think anything about it. She popped a 400 mg Ibuprofen pill when in pain, and the pain lessened for a while.

She continued to lead worship sets and praising her God with her guitar. However, over the course of a few months her condition worsened to the point where she was in severe pain, and she could no longer play her guitar.

Before all this happened to Marcy, the Lord gave her the name: "Set in Praise." Wow, what a name! "Set in Praise" What does this look like? Marcy saw a picture—she was standing with her hands raised and face lifted to the sky in worship. Next she saw herself in the middle of storm still in worship. She didn't know this picture would become her reality, and that she'd grow to a new level in worship.

Marcy was experiencing this great storm in her life and had to make a choice to praise her God anyway in the midst of her pain. She pressed through a difficult season and praised God anyway, without her guitar.

During this time, God taught her what true worship and praise was to Him. She was getting back to the *heart of worship* where it's all about Him. She gave Him more than a song. She gave herself. She worshipped while in pain. I saw her do this, and it is forever etched in my mind.

It was March 2012 at a women's retreat, we stood and worshipped God as a young lady played the keyboard, and Marcy stood and led worship without her guitar. Marcy walked to the middle of the room and stood in the inner circle near eight worshipping women. She praised God, "God, You're so worthy. God, You're highly exalted. God, there is none like You. Be exalted.

Be enthroned in our worship." She lifted both of her arms straight up toward heaven, and then she twirled her arms side to side in a waving motion, praising her God.

I stared at her with amazement with my jaw pointing toward the floor. "How is she doing that?" If you'd seen Marcy earlier that day she was cradling her arm like it was a newborn baby. Now, that arm was straight up in the air. We thought Marcy was healed in that moment, but she wasn't; the pain was still there. She praised her God with all her being that day, holding nothing back not even her painful arm and shoulder. She gave a sacrifice of praise to God.

I wish you could've been there to witness this for yourself. Marcy was truly set in praise and fulfilled the words of the song: "Praise is what I do even when I'm going through" on that day and other days, too. She is such an example to me and to others. When I think about my struggle with endometriosis, and I don't feel like praising God, I'm reminded of my friend Marcy, who—in order to praise God—lifted her throbbing arm that was full of teeth-gritting pain. It motivates and encourages me to do the same.

What happens when your hands, body, voice or feet fail you? Maybe you were a dancer and that's how you worshipped and praised God, and now you can't dance? Maybe you played the tambourine, or you played an instrument like my friend Marcy, and now you can't? Maybe you sang songs of praise to God or you wrote songs about Him, and now you can't? How will you praise Him now? Will you still praise Him anyway?

Will we press through and praise Him because He's still worthy of our worship and praise? Will we give Him more than a song, a dance, a beat, a strum or hand clap? Will we praise Him for what He's already done for us, even without a healing or a cure? Could we find something to praise Him about just "for Him alone?" I hope Marcy's story will encourage and motivate you, too, as it has me, to praise God when you're going through. May you and I be "set in praise."

(Update: Marcy is now pain-free. The painful journey ended August 2012. Her shoulder and arm are back to normal, and she's back to playing her guitar and still worships and praises her God extravagantly. Praise God!)

Here's what I'm asking God...

God, I will bless you while I live. I will lift up my hands in your name, no matter the situation or circumstance or my condition. Cause me to be "set in praise" in the midst of life storms, and let nothing move me from Your presence. It's not based on my feelings but on who You are. You are always worthy to be praised. Come near as I praise You and rest, dwell and abide a while with me. I praise, exalt and adore Your Holy name. I declare I will enter into Your courts with praise. I will praise You with my whole being, holding nothing back, but giving You all of my praise. (Psalm 63:4; 100:4; 144:9).

Here's something to think on...

He tends to linger, abide and dwell where He's being adored and praised. (Psalm 22:3).

Here's a tip to help you stand...

Praise God without props— (no music and no instruments if you're bold) just your voice, your hands, your feet, your heart, your mind, your soul and your spirit. Write on a piece of tape: "Set in Praise," and put it on the bottom of the sole of your shoes or on your hand or another place as a sign that you're *set in praise* no matter what you go through.

LETTER 44

Take Up Your Mat and Walk

"I shall not die, but live, and declare the works of the Lord."
~David (Psalm 118:17).

Dear *Woman*,

What is your mat? I'm not talking about your yoga mat. What's the thing you have been laying on or confined to that might represent an illness, dysfunction or situation? My mat has been this endo illness.

There was a man paralyzed for thirty-eight years, who was confined to a mat. (See John 5:1-13). He parked his mat beside the pool of Bethesda and waited for someone to put him in the water so he could be healed.

Year after year no one helped him, and he remained paralyzed. Until one day, Jesus walked up to him and asked him, "Do you want to be healed?"[59]

He didn't answer Jesus's question, but he gave an excuse and all the reasons why he wasn't healed.

I wonder if this was the first time he'd heard this question or the 38th time he'd heard it.

Whether it was the first time or not, he said, "I have no one to put me in the pool when the water is disturbed, and while I'm trying to get there, someone goes in ahead of me."[60]

Why didn't he ask someone to help him into the pool? Maybe he feared being misunderstood, rejected or ridiculed. So he didn't ask for help.

Jesus said to him, "Get up and take up your mat and walk."[61]

And the man did just that. He got up and walked around carrying his mat, which represented his sickness and disability. He was now holding in his hand the thing that he had been bound to for years. Jesus could have said "Get up and walk," and that's it. But he didn't. He made sure the man picked up the thing, which had labeled him as a sick man, so everyone could see he was no longer confined to his mat and no longer paralyzed.

Now he had a story to tell. Can you see him saying, "You see this mat. Can you believe I laid on this old thing for thirty-eight years? But guess what, this man named Jesus spoke to me and told me to get up."

I imagine him walking by other people that were mat-bound, and their eyes fell upon him, and he shared his story all over again. His story released hope in their hearts for them to be able to walk, too.

While his testimony gave hope to others, it caused an uproar with the Pharisees. They said to the man, "Why are you carrying your mat? It is the Sabbath." His mat story made them so uncomfortable.

But he didn't care. He carried his mat and told them, "The man who healed me — He's the one who told me, 'Pick up your mat and walk.'"[62]

I will follow in the steps of the former paralyzed man and take up my mat of shame, misunderstanding, pain, and disappointments. I will walk in confidence, boldness, joy, peace and comfort. What has tried to define me will be turned into a tool in my hand and a story in my mouth to demonstrate God's mercy, grace and overcoming power. It will become my mat testimony.

What is your mat story? Is it about dealing with an illness or is it about how God restored your marriage? Is it about how God helped you make it through school or provided for you in the tough times? Is it about how you're a survivor of cancer or freed from an addiction? Is it about going through foreclosure and bouncing back, or how you endured the loss of a loved one?

Whatever it is, pick it up and showcase it for all to see that it no longer defines you. It will probably intimidate and make some people uncomfortable. Be bold and courageous, and don't worry about the haters who say, "Why are you sharing that? Why are you making a big deal out of it? You shouldn't share that about your life. You know some things you should keep to yourself."

Don't listen to them; share it anyway, and proclaim it loud and clear for all to hear. It's your story and testimony, and no one can stop you. Remind them who told you to "take up your mat and walk." Walk in strength and might. Walk in confidence and boldness. Walk in certainty and power. Walk in grace and wisdom. Walk in truth and light. Walk along, and share your story (testimony) to all those who will hear.

Others might say, "Wasn't she the one who—" (You can fill in the blank.) You'll respond, "Yes, I am the one, but see I'm walking now."

Others might ask with sincerity, "Hey, tell me about your mat story. What does that mat mean?"

Tell them and watch them be encouraged. Tell them and watch them be comforted. Tell them and watch them be changed. Take up your mat and be a walking billboard. Go forth, and use it as a powerful tool by which you have overcome—to touch lives.

Here's what I'm asking God...

God, I hear you speaking over me, "Take up your mat and walk." You have given me the grace, power and ability to go forth and use that thing (mat) in my life that I was confined to. You let me use it as a testimony of Your goodness and power over my circumstances. I will lift my voice in boldness. May You be glorified as people hear my story. I will proclaim "the good news of righteousness in the great assembly." (Psalm 40:9). I declare the works of the Lord, for He has done great things in my life. (Psalm 118:17).

Here's something to think on...

There's overcoming power in your testimony. (Revelation 12:11).

Here's a tip to help you stand...

Use your mat as a talking piece to share your story. Share it on social media or on a blog. Start an organization or host a meeting. Write an essay, a book or short story and title it "Mat Stories." (I'd love to here your mat stories. Share your endo, cancer, fibromyalgia, lupus, marriage, infertility, singleness, financial freedom and victory-over-abuse stories, and encourage others.) Let our voices combine. #matstories

LETTER 45

Strong Woman

"Strength and honor are her clothing; she shall rejoice in time to come."
~King Lemuel's Mother (Proverbs 31:25).

Dear *Woman*,

Did you know the strongest woman in the world benched 800 pounds and "performed an equipped-bench-press of 600 pounds totaling more than 2000 pounds?"[63] Now, that's one strong woman.

You're one strong woman, too. You bench press daily. It might not be 800-pound weights, but you bench press laundry, groceries, little kids, concerns and cares, patients, casework, housework, classwork, prayers to God, business operations, you name it, all the while dealing with a chronic illness.

Some days are better than others. And those days of feeling down, weak and not wanting to get out of bed don't change or determine or define who you really are: S-T-R-O-N-G: Simply To Rely ON God.

You are one strong sister. At times you might not think or feel like you are strong, but you are. You are a mighty woman of valor. You might feel like Gideon—you don't see yourself as a strong warrior. Gideon was called by God to save his country (Israel) from the hand of the Midianites, but when God called him to this task Gideon didn't see himself as strong.

He said, "O my Lord, how can I save Israel? Indeed my clan is the weakest in Manasseh, and I am the least in my father's house." (Judges 6:15).

God spoke to his purpose, identity, and confidence level, not to his situation or his feelings. You are strong even if you don't feel like it. God is with you, and you will defeat whatever illness, obstacle, or situation that stands in your way.

Or maybe you feel like Samson, you were strong once and a force hard to beat, and then something happened to cause you to lose that strength. Samson revealed that his strength was in his hair and that if it was ever cut he would lose his strength. Soon after revealing this, his hair was cut off, and he was no longer strong.

Maybe it was revealed by you, or someone else, or through a situation where your strength was, and then that thing was cut off, and you're no longer strong. It won't be long before your strength will return to you.

Samson's hair grew back, and he was a strong, mighty man again. Stronger than before. And so will you and I be. We will gain our strength back, and whatever was cut off or pruned from us will grow back and be restored to us. We will be stronger than before.

Be strong because you are. You know where your strength comes from. You're charged up. Strong in your faith. Strong in your character. Strong in your moral behavior. Strong in your integrity. Strong in your convictions. Strong in your examples to others. You go strong. Strong in perseverance. Strong in your mind. Strong in your heart.

You are a strong woman, taking care of a special-needs child or an elderly parent with Alzheimer's, or a husband with cancer. You may be encouraging a friend, who struggles with bulimia, or rescuing children from sex trafficking.

It's nothing for you to bend down, squat and thrust those weights in your life up over your head toward Heaven. For you know God's yoke is easy, and His burden is light. He has equipped you with power and might and made you strong.

Here's what I'm asking God...

God, I will be strong in the power of Your might. I lay aside all weights that try to hold me down and ensnare me. I take up Your yoke, for it is light. Bless my eyes to see myself as You see me—as a woman of valor—and renew my strength. I declare I will be strong and not fear, for I'm clothed with strength.

Here's something to think on...

You are called to be strong and of good courage. (Joshua 1:8).

Here's a tip to help you stand...

Be S-T-R-O-N-G: Simply To Rely ON God. When you feel your strength fading, remember to awake and put on strength each day like a garment and wear it as your favorite outfit. Let strength be your clothing.

Word challenge: create your own acronym for the word "strong."

LETTER 46

Them Fighting Words

"Rush your giant with a God saturated-soul."[64]
~Max Lucado

Dear *Woman*,

Your mama! Those are definitely fighting words. Have you ever seen a fight start because of those words? Those words are used to arouse and aggravate you to wanna jump across the table and deal with the person who said those two hurtful words "Your Mama" (better spoken as 'Yo' Mama' with a definitive head nod).

When I was in high school, it didn't matter if the agitator said, "You're ugly. You're dumb." Those words didn't stick and cause an impact like saying, "Yo Mama." This statement caused even the nicest and sweetest person, to say, "Okay, them are fighting words. Don't you dare talk about my mama." Mama birthed us, cared for us and loves us no matter what. Mama is dear to our hearts, and we'll defend Mama when her name is being chewed up and spewed out by an agitator.

If someone is upset and ready to fight because the one who birthed them is talked about. What will happen when the one who created us, God, is talked about?

The children of Israel were at war with the Philistine army. The army sent out one of its mighty warriors—a giant named Goliath. He taunted the children of Israel. And it was as if he said to the children of Israel, "Yo' God can't stand up against me!"

"No, he didn't. Awwwe Naw it's on now." You'd think the children of Israel would rise up and fight now, but they didn't. The children of Israel listened to the giant's words, and let his words penetrate their hearts and minds. The children of Israel sat prepared for battle, but didn't get into it. Maybe they were waiting for Goliath to throw the first javelin. He never did. Or insult their mamas.

He only hurled words at them, which did more damage than his unthrown javelin. His words paralyzed them with fear and disabled them from fighting. His words were meant to stir up some kind of reaction from the children of Israel to fight, but they didn't. The children of Israel allowed his uncircumcised self to taunt them for forty days and forty nights. How long is too long? When is it enough verbal abuse?

There was no match for Goliath, until a little ruddy, bright-eyed, good-looking boy named David came on the scene carrying a lunch basket to his brothers and overheard Goliath's taunting. This is how I imagine it went down. (See 1 Samuel 17.)

David got to the battle ground and said, "Hey, what's going on guys?" He glanced over on the other side of the hill and saw the nine-foot-nine-inch giant, Goliath, shouting taunts at the children of Israel. Something kindled inside of David, "Who does he think he is? Who is he talking to? Doesn't he know we are the children of the Most High God? He better watch his mouth."

He turned to one of the soldiers, "Tell me, what is the reward for taking him out?"

They answered, "...One of the king's daughter and the man's entire family will be exempted from paying taxes!" (1 Samuel 17:24).

I imagine David speaking to himself, "With God by my side, I can take him. I can use my well-tested tools, the ol' stone-and-slingshot method. He confronted Goliath with courage and boldness.

Goliath insulted and cursed David. And the fight was on.

David pulled out his slingshot and a stone from his side and rushed toward his giant with passion, boldness and might.

"POW!" The stone landed right in the middle of Goliath's forehead, and the nine-foot-nine-inch braggart fell forward to the ground causing the dirt to fly everywhere. David grabbed Goliath's sword and held it up in the air. He looked down at Goliath and let the sword swing downward cutting off Goliath's head, ending his life and his taunting words. His giant's fearful and abusive voice was silenced that day.

Do you have a giant in your life? Has it been taunting you for days or even years—saying all kinds of things that are the equivalent of saying 'yo Mama?' I let my giant (endo) taunt me for years, forget forty days. The children of Israel did better than me. But then I'd had enough, and the fight was on.

What is your slingshot-and-stone method? It is something we've tried and tested before, and it worked on small things. It will work on the big things, too. We've been given a slingshot and a stone, which is the Word of God and His Holy Spirit; it's been tried, tested and proven true. We use it as a mighty sword to fight. We can take down any giant that stands against us and mouths off negative, ungodly and fearful things to us. We can declare the Word of God to our giant, and in return our giant will say to us, "Them are fighting words." Any way it goes, there's going to be a fight.

Our giant will speak things to get a rise out of us, and rise we will—to knock its head off with our slingshot and a stone like David. We will not back down or sit there in our battle gear and not get into the battle. We are Davettas. We've been groomed for battle for years; we've taken out our share of lions and bears. You've overcome an attack on your family and marriage. You've overcome a hard season with dealing with a prodigal or sick child. You've overcome a church split. You've overcome a financial dry season. We've overcome many things.

If we fought and won against the lions and bears, what can this giant do? The only place for a giant to go is down. It must fall, and it will fall. Get ready, unhook your slingshot, grab a stone, and go hard after your giant in faith, believing it will fall and bow down to you. CHARGE!

Here's what I'm asking God...

God, make me bold, courageous and fearless like David to face my giants. I will declare Your Word and who You are to those big things in my life and tear down every thought that exalts itself against the knowledge of You in my life. I will use a slingshot and a stone to defeat my giant, and I will take the sword of the Spirit (Your Word) to cut off its head and silence its voice from ever taunting me again. For I will go in the name of the Lord of heaven's armies.

Here's something to think on...

The Lord will hand over your giant, and all you have to do is kill it and cut its head off. (1 Samuel 17:46 NLT).

Here's a tip to help you stand...

Face your giants: create a paper giant and name it (what are you dealing with that is a giant in your life?) Or line up bottles or cups that represent your giants. Make a slingshot of sticks, pencils or fingers, and use a rock or ping-pong ball or balled-up paper (representing truth, scriptures, inspirational quotes). Take out your giants one by one. Have fun.

Spiritual side: Use the Word (a scripture verse) and the Spirit to fight your giants. Take the sword of the Spirit and cut the giant's head off.

LETTER 47

Fight Like a Lady

"One sure way to win is to fight with faith in your corner."
~Chavos B.

Dear *Woman*,

I fight like a girl. Well, should I say, more like a lady. Every day I enter the boxing ring of life, and the announcers speak, "We have in the pink corner weighing in at 130 pounds, 5' 8," wearing pearls, blue jeans, a ruched turquoise top and black high-heeled boots—more than a conqueror, daughter of the King."

(The crowd of witnesses lean over the balcony of Heaven and cheer.)

"Chavos" aka Sweetheart aka Beautiful." Her husband whistles from the crowd, and she does a little step-and-wave to the crowd as if she's in a Miss America Pageant.

"I-nnnn, the yellow corner, weighing at 176 million plus pounds, wearing pain, fatigue pants, nausea, heavy bleeding, and more-than-normal cramps—"

"Boo, Boo," the crowd hollers.

"Get out the ring," a woman yells.

"The Silent Killer, En-doe-me-tree-o-sis!" the announcer pronounces.

Chavos and Endo walk to the middle of the ring and stare at each other. Endo's look is one of destruction. Chavos's is one of I'm-not-going-down-without-a-kick-in-your-face fight.

The ref says, "Okay, here are the rules: no hitting below the belt. Let's have a good clean fight. Go back to your corners, and come out fighting when the bell rings."

(I dare not turn my back on Endo; it can't be trusted, so I walk backward to my corner with my eyes on Endo).

Ding, Ding...Round One

"It's a slow start at the Arena of Life. They're just dancing out there. No one wants to make the first blow. Ok, Endo throws the first jab, and another."

"It doesn't even seem like the contender Chavos has a desire to fight. She is laying down on the mat. She gets up, and oh my, Endo gave a hard jab again, this time hitting her in the stomach. Oh no, she threw up everywhere. That's not a good sight to see. Folks, we're going to go to a quick bathroom break as they clean up this mess.

"We're back.

"That was a rough round for the contender, I must say that round goes to Endo. What do you think?"

"I agree, Endo meant to cause some pain," says the other announcer.

"Ok, folks. Here we go."

Ding, Ding...Round Two

"Endo comes out swinging and very aggressive this round. It's not wasting any time. Getting the jabs in early.

"Endo delivers a blow below the belt. Chavos is bent over, and she appears to be in a lot of pain. She's crying."

"Boo, Boo, cheater," the crowd yells.

The ref walks over to Chavos to see if she's okay, "Are you okay? Do you need a break?"

She shakes her head to signal to the referee that she's not okay. She wipes the tears from her eyes and fixes her pearls in place around her neck.

The referee walks over to Endo, "Endo, this is a warning, no hitting below the belt."

"Okay, here we go folks. The contender has gathered herself and wiped her tears and..."

Ding, ding...Rounds Three, Four and Five

"Endo throws a left punch, then a right, another right, oh, Endo threw a painful uppercut punch and another painful punch. Endo isn't giving Chavos any breathing room, folks. Is this ref going to stop this fight? The contender tries to fight through the pain, but folks, she seems to be in a lot of discomfort and pain.

"Endo looks like it's going in for the kill. It is on a mission to destroy her. Someone needs to throw in the towel and stop this fight."

Ding, Ding, Ding...

"That was hard to watch, but it's over now...I hope she's okay and fights through this.

"I'm not sure, Endo is a strong opponent. Folks, we'll be back right after this break."

"Welcome back, folks, five rounds have past, and the contender is weak and not fit to fight this battle. The last rounds clearly go to Endo."

"I totally agree with you," says the co-announcer.

Ding, Ding...Round Six

"Let's see if this will be a better round for the contender. It looks like she has received some tips from her coaches.

"Chavos comes out in this round with a right hook to Endo. I believe, this is the first time she's gotten to touch Endo."

(The crowd cheers).

"Endo is taken by surprise with that hit. It didn't expect it from the contender. Endo throws a left hook, then a right.

"Chavos blocks both hits, now defending herself (prayer). Chavos leans in to hit Endo with a powerful right hook and another right hook and another (surgery).

"Folks, I can't believe it, Endo is cut and bleeding. It doesn't look good. That was some cut! We'll take a break, while Endo gets that deep cut checked out and bandaged up.

"Folks, that round went to the contender."

Ding, Ding...Round Seven

"Chavos goes back to her corner to drink what looks like a special smoothie drink. I hope it gives her the strength she needs to fight this next round."

"Yeah, me too. We're told she changed her diet to be in better shape for this match. She switched to eating gluten-free bread for a while. I heard that's all the big rave right now. Let's see if it helps her," says the co-announcer.

"Endo doesn't look too happy about that last round."

Ding, Ding...Round Eight

"Endo strikes Chavos in the stomach several times. Chavos hurries to her corner just barely making it to a gray plastic bag hanging on the post at ring side.

"Folks, her head is totally immersed in the bag, and any fluid and food that was in her stomach is now in that bag.

"She has visited the bag five times throughout this round. She looks horrible.

"Yes, she does. She's looks dehydrated and weak.

"Endo strikes Chavos again. Chavos is too weak to lift her arms to punch back."

"Oh, she's taking a beating out there. Someone needs to stop this fight... this round seems worse than the earlier rounds. She's staggering all over the place. She can't hardly stand up. She swings and totally misses Endo, and runs into the ropes. I can't watch this.

"Wait a minute, folks, something is going on inside the ring. It appears another person just stepped into the ring.

"It's the Lord of Hosts, the King of Kings. He leans over and whispers something to Chavos, and then He just steps inside of her body.

"Looks like she has some help now."

"Is that legal?" the co-announcer asks.

"Well, I'm not sure, but technically it is still one person."

"Oh boy, Endo is in trouble now."

"Let's see how this next round goes."

Ding, Ding...Round Nine

"Okay, folks, in a strange turn of events, it looks like Chavos has regained her composure. She gives Endo a nice uppercut. We have us a match. Oh, she's got Endo in the corner, right jab (prayer), left jab (Ibuprofen), right (Word of God), left (exercising). She will not let up. She is relentless. The ref is trying to break them up.

"She hits it with a right hook (scriptural prayer and declaration). Endo is staggering; it seems to be dazed. Endo is cut up bad. Endo is totally inactive this round. Oh, she hits it again with another right hook (prayer, surgery, the Word, diet). Endo is fighting to keep its balance.

"Folks, Chavos is going in for the kill, she has that look in her eyes. Boom...she delivers a powerful blow—heard throughout the arena. Everyone is standing. The crowd is cheering.

"Endo spins once and staggers but can't regain balance...Endo hits the mat."

"One, two, three, four, five," the Ref counts.

"Endo's trying to get up."

"Six, seven, eight," the Ref counts.

"Endo can't seem to get it together."

"Nine, ten," the Ref counts,

"That's it, folks. It's a knock out. The crowd is going wild."

"Yay, yay, yay!" the crowd yells and cheers.

There'll be a rematch because Endo doesn't know when to give up. I plan to have this fight all over again next month and every month until it leaves me alone. I have gone toe-to-toe with Endo. I'm a fighter, and you are, too. You are relentless and will not back down now or cower before any sickness, situation, challenge, struggle or blows that come your way. Be encouraged and know there are people cheering you on to win each second, hour, day, month and year. And though it's not a pretty fight, you are determined and relentless.

You fight not just for yourself but for others in your same situation. You fight for the generation of women that are coming behind you. You are a champion, more than a conqueror, and you have the battle scars to prove it. I'm cheering for you today. You go, girl. Put your heels on and your dukes up. It's time to fight.

Here's what I'm asking God...

God, You are my Lord, My God—a God of war. You are One who goes with me and fights for me. This battle is not mine, but Yours to fight. Cause me to fight the good fight and fight from a place of victory that I may walk in overcoming power day by day, month after month. Give me your shield of victory. Command victories for me, O Lord. I declare I am more than a conqueror, and I will not fall, for the Lord God Himself fights for me.

Here's something to think on...

God has never lost a fight. He's undefeated, and He fights for you. (Exodus 14:14; Deuteronomy 20:4; Joshua 23:10).

Here's a tip to help you stand...

Put your dukes up and FIGHT: Buy yourself some boxing gloves or print out a picture of some and do some shadow boxing. Picture yourself fighting your illness. Hang up or frame the gloves.

Write an inspirational quote to yourself on a shirt like: I went toe-to-toe with (name the illness or situation), or I fight like a lady against (that illness or situation) or (The illness or situation) got knocked-out. For example, my shirt would say, "I went toe-to-toe with Endo and won."

LETTER 48

Woman of Faith

"O woman, great is your faith! Let it be to you as you desire."
~Jesus (Matthew 15:28).

Dear *Woman*,

You are among a great company of women of faith—women of faith, whose stories are written in a book by the hand of God, women of faith not afraid to break a sweat and strengthen that which remains. You have been added to a list of women of faith throughout history. Women like:

- Sarah, who had faith to conceive when it was impossible
- Rahab, who had faith to hide the two Israelites spies and saved her whole family
- Ruth, who had faith to leave her people and home to go with her mother-in law to a foreign land
- Esther, who had faith to risk her life and go before the king to petition for the life of her people
- Jael, who had faith to invite an evil king into her tent and then kill him, saving her nation
- Dorcas, who had faith to selflessly make clothes for the poor
- The widow woman, who had faith to give her last ounce of food to a man she didn't even know
- Harriet Tubman, who had faith to lead slaves to freedom through an unconventional way

- Kathryn Kuhlman, who had faith to see God move powerfully to heal people
- And You, who have faith to…(What will be written about you as a woman of faith? Oh, I hope one day to read the story of your great faith.)

Women of faith are more than just pretty faces with painted eyelids, nails and lipstick; they stare down and have a face off with doubt and fear. Women of faith take strides of grace and run their race in high heels. They're unstoppable. You're unstoppable. Women of faith are not afraid to cry because they know their tears are precious to God. Women of faith are not void of issues, but full of endurance to get through their issues.

Women of faith are fully alive. Women of faith are good at math and are daily adding to their faith, virtue and kindness. Women of faith have foresight; they see and hope for what is not yet seen. Women of faith laugh without fear of the future; their confidence and assurance is in the Author and Finisher of their faith.[65]

Women of faith—what a good tribe to be a part of and good company to keep. I desire and pray to be a woman of great faith and to be among the company of these great women. And at the end of my life one of the things I would like to be known as is a "woman of faith."

I always thought that to be a woman of great faith meant to have perfect, unwavering faith, but as I look at the stories of people of faith, their journeys of faith weren't perfect. "Christ isn't asking us to believe in our ability to exercise unwavering faith. He is asking us to believe that He is able."[66] I love this quote by Beth Moore. It's so freeing to know that my sometimes-too-often wavering faith doesn't disqualify me from the hope of one day being a woman of great faith. It doesn't disqualify you, either.

You're on the move. You are going from faith to faith. Your faith has been through fiery trials like gold in a furnace. Your faith has run laps around the track of life and back like a great track star. It's endured and persevered and overcome. "And this is the victory that has overcome the world—our faith." (1 John 5:4). We are women of faith on a journey taking one step at a time, trusting and believing and overcoming. I'm glad to be a part of this great company with you. Run your race well, and I'll meet you at the finish line.

Woman of Faith

Here's what I'm asking God...

God, increase my faith in this season of my life. Let me go from faith to faith. I want to be a part of the army of women of faith in the history books of Heaven. Cause me to be a woman of great faith, and grant me what I desire because of faith. I declare I will add to my "faith—virtue, to virtue—knowledge, to knowledge—self-control, to self-control—perseverance, to perseverance—godliness, to godliness—brotherly kindness, and to brotherly kindness—love." (2 Peter 1:5).

Here's something to think on...

The just live by faith. Faith comes by hearing and hearing by the Word of God. (Romans 1:17; 10:17).

Here's a tip to help you stand...

Add to your faith daily. Attend a women's conference in your area or read a book about the great women of faith in our history.

LETTER 49

The End of Endo

> "Endo must go. Endo must end. Endo must be cured."
> ~Chavos B.

Dear *Woman*,

My aunt was shot and slipped into a comatose state for three months. I'm talking about my Aunt Flo. What happened, you ask? She was shot by Lupron Depot. Have you heard that name before? It's a medication that stops the menstrual cycle for a while. Some of the side effects were annoying and uncomfortable, but I would take a hot flash any day over pain, cramps, nausea, and fatigue.

Aunt Flo was asleep and off in dreamland in a faraway place called pre-menopause-ville. It felt like she was on a very long vacation, and I didn't miss her at all. I didn't have to deal with her crazy evil pets, 'Pain and Cramps.' There was no dancing to her moods. I didn't have to carry her heavy luggage, and there was no more war with my stomach and food, but a peace treaty was safely in place. I had strength in my legs and was free to move in and out as I pleased, no longer homebound.

My prayers of "God, please stop my period. God, please let this end. God, please make this all go away" were finally answered. The endo-storms had ceased for a while, and for the first time in ten years I felt like a normal girl, well woman. My life no longer looked like misery, but it was good times. I soaked up all the time of Aunt Flo's absence, forgetting all about her and enjoying life. I felt like a teenager in an empty house, one whose parents had gone on a vacation. It was time to party. There was no need to gear-up for her visits and count down the days until she'd return. Aunt Flo wasn't coming for a while.

I knew the three months would go by fast, and she would soon awake from her comatose state and come knocking at my door saying, "I'm back. Did you miss me?"

"No, not at all." I'd reply, "But that all depends on if you've changed your behavior. Are you going to be different this time? Did you have an encounter while you were sleeping that made you nicer and sweeter?"

There must be an end to endo. A stop to it forever. Hearing: "There is no cure," is hard. It's hard for me to believe that there's no pill, vitamin or something to make it stop like a cold, flu or headache. It's different. Why is this illness so different? Why hasn't anyone found a cure?

I wish I knew the cure. I've prayed and asked God to release wisdom and to reveal the cure to medical experts and scientists. Maybe if we knew how we got it, then we could know how to cure it. I wish I knew how to end endo and other chronic illnesses, not just for me, but for you, too. I wish I knew the secret to unlocking the research, but I don't. I wish I could tell you that endo or cancer or lupus or fibromyalgia will end soon.

I've told you what I don't know, but what do I know? Hope. I have hope for a cure—if not for me, at least for my unborn daughters, my friends' daughters, my niece and my little cousins. Hope for a future without endo. Hope for a future without chronic illnesses at all. A hope that God will unlock the cure and release it to researchers, and they will discover it.

Until then, let's continue to believe and hope for an end to endo, cancer, lupus, sickle-cell anemia, fibromyalgia, rheumatoid arthritis, and all other illnesses. Let's mobilize, strategize, and lift our voices together through prayer, podcasts, blogs, social media, forums, support groups, marches and speeches. Let's fight to end endo for our daughters, nieces and friends. Everything has an end. Every bad thing must come to an end, and something new will begin. Expect an end, and look for the start of the new.

Here's what I'm asking God...

God, You are the Alpha and Omega, the Beginning and the End. Will You bring an end to endometriosis, cancer, lupus, fibromyalgia and all other chronic illnesses? Reveal Your thoughts, ideas and plans about how to cure these diseases to scientists and researchers. Give them ears to hear and hearts to receive and minds to understand that You know the answer.

They can try all day long to find the cure, but unless You, O God, illuminate their paths and minds, it will never come to pass. You know what it will take to heal it. It was healed when Jesus, said, "It is finished," on the cross. So be it!

Let there be an end to chronic illnesses. Let the finished work of the cross be manifested in my body and the body of my endo-sisters and those who deal with other illnesses. I declare the Lord sees the end from the beginning, and my end looks good.

Here's something to think on...

Gladness and good years will match the amount of sadness and bad years.
(Psalm 90:15).

Here's a tip to help you stand...

A Minute To Write It (60 seconds): Set your timer for one minute and write on: 'what does the world without endo (name your chronic illness) look like?'

LETTER 50

Worship in the Warfare

> "Whenever we are faced with any calamity such as war, plague, or famine, we can come to stand in your presence..."
> ~King Jehoshaphat (2 Chronicles 20:9 NLT).

Dear *Woman*,

What if—in the midst of war—the US Army sent out singers first instead of soldiers? We would look at them like they were crazy, and the rest of the world would think we've lost our minds. They might even mock and laugh at us saying, "Look, they sent out singers. Ha, singers. How foolish. Where are their soldiers? How can singers fight battles? Singers don't win battles, soldiers do." They better not let the children of Israel hear that, because this is exactly what they did.

The children of Israel found themselves in yet another battle. It appears they were always in a war except for the time of King Solomon's reign. This time, King Jehoshaphat was surrounded by the Ammonites and other nations, and he inquired and prayed to God about the war.

God answered him: "Do not be afraid nor dismayed because of this great multitude, for the battle is not yours, but God's. Tomorrow go down against them." (See 2 Chronicles 20:15-16).

King Jehoshaphat and the children of Israel worshipped God while in the midst of the battle. How could they worship? Why did they worship in the middle of a war? They worshipped because time after time they had experienced effective results that came from their worship. It was a proven warfare strategy. While other armies picked up swords and shields and went to war first, the king and the children of Israel chose to worship first.

"And when he had consulted with the people, he appointed singers unto the Lord, and that should praise the beauty of holiness, as they went out before the army, and to say, Praise the Lord; for his mercy endures forever."

(2 Chronicles 20:21 KJV).

As they entered the enemy's area with songs in their mouths and praise in their hearts, the Lord caused a spirit of confusion to break out in the enemy's camp, and the enemy turned on themselves and fought each other. They completely destroyed themselves. And when the Israelite army reached the battle zone, they saw dead bodies everywhere.

The children of Israel's worship and praise to God defeated their enemies. They spent days collecting the spoils, which included an abundance of valuables, clothing and jewelry from their enemies. This is a glimpse of what singing and praising God can do in our lives and to our enemies. It will give us victory and provision. The children of Israel's approach to war is a great blueprint and inspiration for us and how we can respond in our personal wars.

I've worshipped while in the midst of war. I had just finished vomiting after getting out of the shower. I was in the heat of the raging endo war-zone in my bathroom. Bullets and grenades weren't flying, but waves of nausea, cramps, and everything else that normally comes with endo were. I'd normally get down and depressed and go through the mental exercise of: "Why am I going through this? I'm tired of this. God please stop this," on and on until I fall asleep.

But I didn't do that. This time was different. Instead I lifted up my hands and started to worship. I reached for my cell phone and turned on one of my favorite songs "Our God" recorded by Chris Tomlin, and continued to worship. I worshipped beyond my symptoms and declared,

"You're the God of Creation
You're the God that gives life
You're the God that works miracles
You're the great physician

Worship in the Warfare

> *Rise with healing in your wings*
> *And heal all disease!"* [67]

I sensed God's manifest presence strong as I worshipped in the bathroom war-zone. I couldn't comprehend how I'd shifted from vomiting to worshipping just like that; I know it was God's grace. I often think about that time, and to this day I don't understand why I didn't ball up on the floor like I'd always done before. Whenever my husband heard the infamous gagging sound coming from my mouth, he would stop what he was doing and come to the rescue and pray for me. But not this time. It was different. I worshipped instead.

God taught me how to worship in warfare on that day, and nothing can take that from me. I know now what I'm capable of doing in the midst of an endo war-zone. I really felt like I was "more than a conqueror." I know it's not about feelings, but on that day, in the endo battle I came into the revelation of the *more-than-a-conqueror identity*. That day I asked God for compensation for all the years I've dealt with endo and time stolen from me by the enemy. That day I declared war on endo and sickness. That day was the wrong day to mess with me. I conquered and stood as a worshipping warrior.

Are you in a war right now? If so, worship and praise is a fierce weapon in the midst of your battle. You are a worshipping warrior. As you lift your voice and hands in praise to your God, things will begin to move and shake. You know what it takes to give sacrifices of praise and worship. Your worship confuses your situation. It says, "Wait a minute. I thought she was down, in pain, sick, angry, hurt." You name it.

And you might very well be, but you're a worshipping warrior. You know, warriors get hurt all the time, but that doesn't stop them from fighting. And we are worshipping warriors, and our battles won't stop us from singing to God.

We will worship our Lord, who is the Lord of heaven's army. We will worship our Lord, who trains our hands for war and gives us the victory and the power to advance towards the gates of the enemy. We will worship our Lord, for He is a man of war and fights for you and me.

Here's what I'm asking God...

God, my first response to warfare and any battle in my life is to complain, self-evaluate and over-analyze. Let there be a shift in my mindset and attitude toward warfare. Cause my first response to be praise and worship. This isn't natural for me, so I need Your Spirit to give me grace and retrain my behavior. Let all the spoils owed to me from previous battles and wars in my life, be released and given to me in this season. Thank you for teaching me how to properly wage war. I declare I will stand and see Your victory in my life, O Lord.

Here's something to think on...

"The Lord is a man of war..." and He will train your hands for war.
(Psalm 144:1; Exodus 15:3*a*).

Here's a tip to help you stand...

In the heat of your battle, turn on some praise and worship music, lift your hands and worship in your own unique way. Watch what happens.

When there is a war of any kind, there are spoils. There are spoils to be collected by you with your name on them. They belong to you because you've fought and battled and warred. Claim your spoils; ask for compensation from past battles and wars.

LETTER 51

Most Wanted

"And I will put enmity between you and the woman, and between your seed and her Seed; He shall bruise your head, and you shall bruise His heal."
~God (Genesis 3:15).

Dear *Woman*,

I'm armed and virtuous. Courageous and dangerous. You are, too. We're on the Most-Wanted List—not America's, but the kingdom of darkness's. The poster reads, "Wanted for shining light in dark places. Beware: she is a threat to society and salt on the earth. Don't listen to what she has to say. She was once a child of darkness, but now she's a child of the light. She's armed with powerful weapons and with the authority to trample on serpents and over the power of her enemy. No weapons of any kind can work against her. Be on the lookout, but please don't engage her; she is very dangerous."

The America's Most-Wanted List has some of the most notoriously dangerous criminals known for committing some the most horrible crimes that cause hurt, damage, and pain in the lives of others, which makes them a powerful threat to the peace and safety of society. We'd expect them to be on the list so we can beware and watch out for them.

But for law-abiding citizens like us, regular ol' women, girls, wives, mothers, daughters, students, and sisters. We wouldn't expect to see our names on a Most-Wanted List. Right? Wrong! The kingdom of darkness has the opposite on its Most-Wanted List. It has the most notorious righteous believers, committing acts of kindness, causing light to break out wherever they go, and speaking words of comfort and encouragement to people. Life givers, peace-makers, giant killers, cross-bearers, called out ones. You are dangerous, disastrous and hazardous to the kingdom of darkness. You violently and aggressively pursue the Kingdom of God and His righteousness. Your mantra is "The kingdom suffers violence, and I'm violent, and I will take it by force." You are the light of the world, and darkness hates your light.

So, you see why you're on the Most-Wanted List? What are you notorious (known) for that gets the attention of your enemy? Are you known as: A mother who loves, nurtures and trains her children. A wife who is virtuous, resourceful, honoring and supporting of her husband as a Proverbs 31 wife. A business woman, who works with excellence and grace, walks in wisdom and gives to those in need. A nurse, who cares for her patients with great care, loving-kindness and tenderness. A teacher, who instructs and trains her students to be their best and prepares them to succeed. A teenager, who walks in purity keeping herself for her wedding day. An athlete, who is skilled on and off the court, beating your body daily. A police officer, who lives as a living sacrifice, showing meekness in power and subject to a higher authority. A politician, who desires to see a government truly trust God and be a nation under God. A lawyer, who loves true justice and takes her cue from the Just One. A pastor, who has a heart after God and feeds the sheep on the knowledge of God. A doctor, who acknowledges God as the great physician in her ways of practicing medicine and faith, who believes healing and miracles are real. A musician, whose music inspires, provokes, and encourages people to forget about their problems. A comedian, who's on a mission to give a dose of laughter to people everywhere. A counselor, who is slow to speak and quick to listen giving timely advice and coached daily by the Wonderful Counselor. An artist, who creates and designs beautiful things for the world to see. A model, who sets an example of what true beauty looks like from the inside out. An actor, who takes directions from an ancient script. A missionary, who is selfless and leaves all to pour out love and hope to others. A photographer, who shows fearfully and wonderfully made things through a different lens. A writer, who writes words of inspiration, comfort, exhortation and encouragement, that touches the heart, changes the mind and heals the soul. A speaker whose words impact people and transform lives.

The thing you're known for will be used for God's glory. And when we function in the full potential of our purpose, shining our light for Christ everywhere and excelling in our area of influence, the kingdom of darkness gets antsy and scared. You've become a powerful threat to the kingdom of darkness because you are children of the Kingdom of Light.

The kingdom of darkness must try to take us out like King Saul tried to do with David. David was a threat to King Saul's kingdom and ended up on his Most-Wanted List because David was successful, killing his ten thousands while Saul only his thousands, and he was chosen and anointed by God to be the next King and replace Saul.

You're called and anointed, and your enemy will try to stop you before you can mobilize, implement change, make new laws, overthrow systems and structures and replace them with something new and better. But the enemy's schemes won't work at all. You're a notorious believer empowered to be a blessing, an influencer and a gift to your community, your family, your city and your nation. You're a great asset to God's kingdom work.

Here's what I'm asking God...

God, the kingdom suffers violence, and the violent ones take it by force. Release Your kingdom force in me to pursue the enemy, for You have given me the authority and power to trample him under my feet. Let Your light shine bright in me and dispel the darkness, and everywhere my feet walk may it be territory claimed for Your kingdom. I declare I am armed with the power from my God and dangerous to the kingdom of darkness. I will chase my enemies and catch them; I will not stop until they are conquered. (Psalm 18:37 NLT).

Here's something to think on...

There's a treasure inside of you ready to be revealed to the world.
(2 Corinthians 4:7).

Here's a tip to help you stand...

What do you want to be notorious (known) for/as? Write some words or phrases that come to your mind. Then use those words and phrases to create a Most-Wanted poster on your computer or by hand. Mount it as a memento to show you're a threat to the kingdom of darkness and asset to the kingdom of light.

LETTER 52

Victorious Woman

> "I will go with you. But you (Barak) will receive no honor in this venture, for the Lord's victory over Sisera will be at the hands of a woman."
> ~Deborah (Judges 4:9 NLT).

Dear *Woman*,

You were built to win. You don't back down. You keep at it again and again. You know how to win. You might get scrapes, scars, bumps and bruises, but you've endured through the illness, the pain, the sadness, the shame. You and I are victorious.

You've been through and fought many battles and experienced some defeats, but you know the ingredients for victory, just like you know the ingredients for your favorite chocolate cake or another special dish. You know what it takes to make a great-tasting dish. So it is, when it comes to winning.

You are victorious because you think like Christ; you let His mind be in you. You discipline unruly thoughts like a cowboy lassoing a wild calf, and you bring those thoughts into submission to Christ.

You are victorious because you are a woman of the Word, whereby you renew your mind daily.[68] You seek to know the mind of God and His thoughts, receiving divine strategies for your life and others'. You use the Word of God as a weapon, a mighty sword to fight lies, bad reports, doubts and unbelief. You're an expert swordswoman.

You are victorious because you lift up the banner of the Lamb's blood. You know there is nothing more powerful or strong enough to penetrate it.

You apply it like war paint before the battle. It acts like a repellant; it weakens the tactics and power of your enemy. It helps us fight the lies, giants and sicknesses, oh my!

There were times, too many to mention, where I felt defeated. Endometriosis was like a 500-pound weight sitting on my life. I didn't feel victorious at all. I felt like a failure, a wimp and a loser. It was as if endo said, "You can't beat me. Matter of fact, you will never beat me. You're defeated." I'd nod in agreement and with my actions, raise the white flag of surrender.

I've come to understand that I am built to win, that I'm victorious—even with my scars, scrapes, wounds and bruises. I would've never known I was built to win if I didn't have to fight and if there was no opposition or struggle in my life. There's no wimp or loser here, not anymore. Endo has made me stronger and taught me how to fight and win.

I know God is with me. I know I can win. I know I have the victory. Defeat is not in my DNA, and neither is it in yours. Here's a song that would make a great battle-cry. It goes like this,

> *"The Lord of Hosts has given me victory*
> *I will storm the gates of the enemy*
> *I hold the shield of victory*
> *To overcome any battle*
> *I know the winning recipe*
> *The enemy is under my feet*
> *I have the victory!"* [69]

I believe victory is mine, and it's yours, though it may seem contrary to our visible situation. The truth is victory belongs to me. The truth is the Lord gives His people victory. The truth is the war is rigged in our favor, and we will win. It's a done deal.

And since it's a done deal, and the battle is rigged in my favor, I can declare, "Victory! Victory today, tomorrow and beyond will forever be mine. I will stand and tell endo and any other disease, emotion, poverty, hopelessness, anger, jealousy, whatever comes against me to get behind me."

Do you believe you have the victory? Do you know that victory is yours? You and I have been given a shield of victory from the Lord of heaven's armies. Who or what can stand against that shield? I think about Captain America's shield and how it was made out of an impenetrable, strong metal. Nothing or no one can destroy that shield. His shield protected him from bullets, knives and blows. How much more is the shield of victory we've been given to carry into battle with us?

Victory is yours. Tell whatever is coming against you to get behind you. Because victory is yours! Whatever that "thing" (illness, trial, suffering) is, it has made you stronger. You are a winner. Your battle stories will encourage and help generations to come. Let's go forth like a mighty, victorious company into battle with our scars, with our swords, with our Savior's blood as war paint and with His shield of victory. And lift up our voices in a battle-cry of VICTORY! Go in the name of the Lord. Go, dear Victorious Woman.

Dear Woman

Here's what I'm asking God...

God, let the shout of victory be in my mouth. For you have given me the ingredients to win and overcome the battles I face. You have given me the victory over my enemies, giants, sickness, depression, fear, loneliness, (name more here), and not a single one of these things will be able to stand up to me. Thank You for the mind of Christ, Your Word, which is my sword, the Blood of Jesus and the shield of Victory. I wait quietly before You God, for my victory comes from You. I declare You protect me from trouble and surround me with songs of victory. (See Joshua 10:8; Psalm 62:1; 32:6-8.)

Here's something to think on...

The Lord gives you victory and His shield of victory is yours.
(Psalm 18:35; 44:7 NLT).

Here's a tip to help you stand...

Have a victory celebration every time you endure. No matter how small. What will your battle-cry be? Raise your voice in your battle-cry. Make yourself a shield out of paper, metal, wood or whatever you want. Create it as a representation of the shield of victory you've been given.

Notes

1. Taken from Turn My Mourning Into Dancing by Henri J Nouwen Copyright © 1994 by Henri J Nouwen. Used by permission of Thomas Nelson. www.thomasnelson.com. All rights reserved.
2. Romans 8:28 NLT
3. Excerpt from THE LITTLE PRINCE by Antoine de Saint-Exupery. Copyright 1943 by Houghton Mifflin Harcourt Publishing Company. Copyright (c) renewed 1971 by Consuelo de Saint-Exupery, English translation copyright © 2000 by Richard Howard. Used by permission of Houghton Mifflin Harcourt Publishing Company. All rights reserved.
4. 2 Corinthians 3:17
5. "Break Every Chain." Grace. Peformed by Tasha Cobbs. Written by William Reagan. Artist: Tasha Cobbs. EMI Gospel (EGS), Copyright © 2009 United Pursuit. Used by permission. All rights reserved.
6. John 8:28
7. Proverbs 18:22
8. Song of Solomon 2:4
9. 2 Corinthians 12:8
10. 2 Corinthians 12:9
11. "Take Me To The King: Medley I Surrender All." Best Days. Written by Kirk Franklin. Performed by Tamlea Mann. Copyright © 2012 Aunt Gertrude Music Publishing Llc. (BMI) (adm. at CapitolCMGPublishing.com) All rights reserved. Used by permission.
12. 2 Samuel 9:13
13. Psalm 16:11
14. Taken from the American Society of Reproductive Medicine (ASRM) patient education booklet, Endometriosis: Does It Cause Infertility? Revised 2012. Used with permission.
15. Taken from the NCHS 2006-2010 report. Used with permission.
16. Genesis 18:10 NLT
17. Taken from a blog post by Joyce Meyer. Used by permission Joyce Meyer Ministries. All rights reserved.
18. Psalm 84:11
19. Genesis 1:26
20. Matthew 7:7
21. 2 Samuel 22:30; Psalm 18:29
22. Zephaniah 3:17
23. Nehemiah 8:10
24. Mark 4:38
25. Psalm 121: 5-6
26. 1 Peter 5:7

27. Quote inspired by Benjamin Franklin's "when in doubt, don't" quote.
28. Mark 9:14-24 NLT
29. Galatians 5:22
30. Proverbs 16:32; 25:28
31. Zephaniah 3:17
32. Hebrews 4:16
33. Proverbs 31:25
34. Proverbs 31:26
35. John 15:14-15
36. Hebrews 4:13
37. Psalm 139:7
38. Genesis 16:13
39. Leviticus 23:3
40. Cat o' nine tails, Wikipedia, http://en.m.wikipedia.org/wiki/Cat_o'_nine_tails, accessed on June 8, 2014.
41. Isaiah 53:5
42. Isaiah 49:16
43. "God's Thoughts" written by Chavos Buycks © 2015 All rights reserved.
44. Isaiah 55:9
45. "What A Friend We Have In Jesus." Lyrics by Joseph M. Scriven 1855. Composed by Charles C. Converse. Song in public domain and may be used without permission.
46. "He Touched Me." Written by William J Gaither. Copyright © 1992 Hanna Street Music (BMI) (adm. at CapitolCMGPublishing.com) All rights reserved. Used by permission.
47. Isaiah 66:14
48. "Free to Be" song written by Chavos Buycks © 2015 All rights reserved.
49. John 11:43
50. John 11:44
51. Psalm 23
52. Psalm 23:2
53. MERE CHRISTIANITY by CS Lewis © copyright CS Lewis Pte Ltd 1942, 1943, 1944, 1952.
54. Matthew 14:33
55. Mark 4:41; Luke 8:25
56. "It Is Well with My Soul" by Horatio G Spafford is public domain and may be used without permission.
57. Psalm 3:3 KJV
58. "Praise Is What I Do." Written by William Murphy III Copyright © 2008 M3m Music (BMI) Lilly Mack Publishing (BMI) (adm. at CapitolCMGPublishing.com) All rights reserved. Used by permission.
59. John 5:7 CJB
60. John 5:7 CJB
61. John 5:8 CJB

Notes

62. John 5:11 CJB
63. Wikipedia, http://en.wikipedia.org/wiki/Becca_Swanson accessed on Feb. 2014
64. Taken from Facing Your Giants: The God Who Made a Miracle Out of David Stands Ready to Make One Out of You by Max Lucado Copyright © 2008 by Max Lucado. Used by permission of Thomas Nelson. www.thomasnelson.com. All rights reserved.
65. Proverbes 31:25 NLT; Hebrews 12:2
66. Taken from Breaking Free: The Journey, The Stories by Beth Moore Copyright © 2009 by Beth Moore. Duplicated and used by permission of Life Way www.lifeway.com. All rights reserved.
67. "You Are" song written by Chavos Buycks Copyright © 2013 All rights reserved.
68. Romans 12:1-2
69. "Shield of Victory" song written by Chavos Buycks Copyright © 2014 All rights reserved.

Top Supporters List

Special thanks and recognition to those who pre-ordered the book.

Hubby (Garry Buycks Jr.)
Jacqueline Buycks
Jennifer (Jenny Jenfo) Davenport
Robert III & Autumn Tribitt
Latora Sojourner
Others who didn't want to be mentioned.☺

Acknowledgments

Special thanks:

To my Heavenly Father, for helping and giving me your grace to make it month after month during this season of my life. For the grace and strength to write and turn around the bad for good. My Lord Jesus, You are the one who has kept my mind and life. You are my Great Physician! Holy Ghost, you help me write. You're the best Holy Ghost writer ever. Thanks for the inspiration and words.

To my husband Garry, my lover, aka Boaz. You are truly a gift from the Father above. We've experienced the part of our vows "in sickness and in health" over and over. And you've honored that part of our vows faithfully. I know it hasn't been easy or by your strength, but by God's strength and His grace. Thank you for the ten years of love, support, prayers, service and caring for me during the worse days of my menstrual cycles and days of recovering from surgeries. Your love and selfless humble service toward me during those times were overwhelming. Thank you for loving me like Christ does. I love you dearly!

To my mother, thank you for your love, declaring the word of the Lord over me in the midst of my doubt and unbelief. You always caused me to see the brighter side of this disease and to know that it will not always be this way. You are a prayer warrior. I am blessed to have a mother like you. Thank you for interceding on my behalf. Also, thank you for helping finish the first draft of this book: Praise God for your fast fingers.

To my sister, Chavonna, thank you for that conversation that changed my life in 2009. It is because of you I gained understanding and insight into what was going on in my body. And thank you for having a listening ear and providing a solution. I love you sissy!

To my Granny, thank you for your love, care and teaching me how to pray and put God first. Thank you for your words of wisdom and encouragement. You're the sweetest, funniest, and wittiest Granny I know.

To my mentors, thank you for your love, support, encouragement, intercession, correction, and for seeing the call of God on my life. Thank you for pushing me to be all that God destined me to be. You've been iron in my life to sharpen me to for the Master's use.

To my literary mentor, Apostle Johnson, thank you for helping me better understand my call as a prophetic writer, for the words of Lord spoken over me, prayers, the accountability sessions and mentoring calls and for Voices of Christ Literary Ministry. I have been richly blessed by your ministry.

To the Friends of Esther Staff, the best group of girlfriends a girl could ask for: thank you for your kindness and support toward me each month during my Endo episodes. You helped me overcome shame that comes with this disease. Thank you for the visit in the hospital before my surgery and for the food. That meant so much to me. Thank you for your faith and encouraging words month after month. It has gotten me through when I felt like giving up. You all wouldn't let me give up. You take me before the feet of Jesus in prayer. You all are dear to my heart.

To my friends (FoFs): Thank you for your prayers, friendship, words of comfort, laughs, and answering my emergency 911 texts during that time of the month. I'm so glad you are in my life.

To my writing pal: Isabel, you are a Godsend, thank you for your prayers, intercessions and encouragement, accountability, feedback, and motivation to help me press through to complete this book. I'm so glad our paths crossed three years ago in a writing class.

To my OBGYN, Dr Lofton (I'm blessed to have a doctor like you) and the medical staff at Midwest Women's Clinic, thank you for your care, support and excellent service during this journey with endo.

To my Editor, Teresa Crumpton, MFA, thank you for your coaching, training, advice, prayers, editorial critique and professional skills to make my words better. You are a God treasure. I so enjoyed working with you on this book.

To Kathy, Barbara, Sherrie, Jackie and Dr. D, thank you for taking time to proofread my book. I appreciate your sweet hearts and your feedback.

To Endo, thank you for totally interrupting my life and giving me a story to share with others. I have become stronger because of you.

About the Author

Chavos Buycks is a wife, creativepreneur (creative entrepreneur), and an author who desires to comfort, exhort, edify and equip others in their purposes. She is a Stage IV Endo fighter and founder of EWWI (Encouraging Women With Illnesses) a faith-based support group. She serves on staff as a media specialist for an international women's ministry. She also leads a writers' group in her area.

Chavos Buycks shares her heart and home with her husband, Garry, in the Midwest. Her life is a letter written by God and read by man. You can find out more about her at www.DearWomanBook.com.

What's Next

Join the *Dear Woman Letters of Hope* challenge every Wednesday. Check the website (www.dearwomanbook.com) for more details.

Nominate a friend to receive a *Dear Woman Hope Package* via the website.

If you enjoyed *Dear Woman*, check out the *Dear Woman workbook* coming soon.

Connect with the author via:
Twitter: @ewwigroup
Facebook/EWWIGROUP
Email: ewwigroup@gmail.com

www.ingramcontent.com/pod-product-compliance
Lightning Source LLC
Chambersburg PA
CBHW052017290426
44112CB00014B/2276